Send
Me

PRAISE FOR SEND ME

"I could not put the book down. For in it you will meet a man who allowed his heart to be broken by the needs of throw-away children in Constanta, Romania … follow in the steps of Hud Staffield and be inspired to listen for God's call on your life."

— **Greg Ogden**, Redeployed Pastor and author of *Discipleship Essentials*

"When God guided him, Hudson listened. In *Send Me*, Hudson shares a heart-breaking, challenging journey that reminds us that God is always with us; equipping us through every trial, no matter how difficult and rocky the path. This book is a triumph, one that will encourage every reader to rely on God, even in the worst of circumstances."

— **Ramona Richards**, author of *My Mother's Quilts, Secrets of Confidence,* and *Burying Daisy Doe*

"I love nothing better than a good story … especially one that's true. Hud Staffield's page-turning account of how God brought him to the aid of the lost children of Romania's orphanages will stay with you long after you turn the last page … and inspire you to step out in faith when the Spirit calls."

— **Carla Laureano**, award-winning author of *London Tides* and *Provenance*

"The book [speaks] to me on multiple levels – business, ministry, and of course personal in regards to all kinds of things about relationships, faith, waiting on God and not lighting one's own fires, being wise as a serpent and innocent as a dove, tough and humble, proactive and patient, bold and gentle. Very inspiring to see this all worked out … Thank you for writing this book."

— **Greg Davis**, former pastor of Saratoga Federated Church

Send Me

To Find and Restore
the Lives of Lost
and Forgotten
Children

Hudson Staffield

Dedication

For Ribana …
and all the others for whom we were too late.

Acknowledgments

I offer many thanks for the following people and groups, without whom this journey—and this book—would not have happened:

- To Greg Ogden, whose questions awakened in me the Spirit's quiet whispers telling me to go.
- To Adi, without whose friendship there would be no House of New Life.
- To the Holy Trinity Baptist Church, Constanta, Romania, whose members sheltered us, loved us, and whose witness grew our faith. I have to also acknowledge the support of our church in Saratoga. Their members have never wavered in supporting us with their prayers, ministry partners, and financial support.
- To the indomitable Chi Rho staff of the House of New Life, the women and men who came to love, care for, and serve the least of the least, because they love the children.
- And to my wife, Cynthia who stayed home and let me go, even when the challenges in our family were daunting; who then came along with me to be what she always is the delight of everyone who meets her: Romanians, church members, Chi Rho staff, and especially the children.

Now the word of the Lord came to me, saying,

"Before I formed you in the womb I knew you,
And before you were born, I consecrated you;
I have appointed you as a prophet to the nations."
Then I said, "Oh, Lord God!
Behold, I do not know how to speak,
Because I am a youth."
But the Lord said to me,
"Do not say, 'I am a youth,'
Because everywhere I send you, you shall go,
And all that I command you, you shall speak.
Do not be afraid of them,
For I am with you to save you," declares the Lord.

Then the Lord stretched out His hand and touched my mouth, and the Lord said to me,

"Behold, I have put My words in your mouth."

—Jeremiah 1:4-9

Introduction

I will not leave you as orphans;
I am coming to you.

—John 14:18

Certain movies are iconic; everyone remembers them. We remember them because of a particular visual or a line in the dialogue that touches on any one of a range of our emotions—for example, scenes of comedy, tragedy, vindication, revenge, or love fulfilled, just to name a few. Thereafter those films become personal, and we never forget them.

I have a habit of going back to look at certain movies over and over again. I have a close friend who chides me for this habit; she thinks I'm wasting my time. She doesn't understand that for me, revisiting a favorite movie can evoke the same pleasure as enjoying a favorite restaurant, rereading a favorite book, seeing again those we love most, or returning to a favorite place.

One of my favorites to revisit is Steven Spielberg's wonderful film *Empire of the Sun*. Yet I can't bring myself to watch the entire movie from beginning to end. This is because I so closely identify with the protagonist in the story; the portrayal of his experiences leaves me with too great a sense of sadness and futility. After watching the opening scenes, I usually skip ahead to the end. Each time I see it, the scene at the end of the movie touches me deeply. I am always brought to tears.

The story is of a little boy, Jim, who is living the privileged life of a British expatriate in colonial Singapore. "Suo Gan" is the movie's musical theme. It's a traditional Welsh lullaby commonly known as "The Mother's Prayer." The opening scene soars visually and musically as we are introduced to the theme as a boys' choir performs this magnificent score, the music resounding beautifully, as it can only in the vaulted ceilings of a baroque cathedral. The little boy has the part of the solo, but everyday life intervenes as we see him annoying the choir director and his Chinese nanny for his lack of attention to the music.

When the Japanese invade the territory at the opening of WWII, Jim is separated from his parents in the ensuing chaos, and he becomes a prisoner in an internment camp. Along with the other unfortunate British expatriates, he suffers cruelty, deprivation, hunger, and loneliness. But he's a resilient little boy, and he manages to survive his years of imprisonment, despite the starvation and neglect, by attaching himself to surrogate parental figures and using his wits. Nevertheless, by the end of the war, he no longer looks out at the world through the eyes of a child.

Once the war is over, Jim is placed in a relocation center for abandoned or orphaned children. Isolated among many other displaced children, he finally loses hope of ever returning to the life he idealizes and exaggerates but that in truth he can barely remember. Vague recollections of the softness and gentleness of a mother have become fewer and fewer until, at last, all his feelings have disappeared. Jim is an empty shell, a small human figure so numb to his surroundings he has disappeared into an imaginary fog. His eyes barely flicker awareness.

Then we see the nuns and the volunteers of the relocation center clap their hands, and as they have been taught to do, the children reflexively form into rows for another viewing by a new group of parents looking for their lost children. All the participants, children and parents, are seen looking about with expectant expressions on their faces, trying to overcome the dread of being disappointed as they search for the survivors of the past four years.

And so unfolds the scene for which Spielberg has been preparing us from the opening of the movie. Some of the parents at last see their children among the lost and cry out their names in unrestrained joy. The children run from the group and into their parents' arms, restored. But Jim can't see them because he isn't looking. He stares out from his fog in disbelief, angry at the joyful confusion disturbing his solitude.

Now the musical score begins to play the "Suo Gan" lullaby again, as it did when the story opened, and we watch as his parents begin to move slowly among the remaining unidentified children. Jim's mother suddenly stops and puts her hand to her mouth, shocked. Recognizing him, she silently mouths his name. Jim still doesn't see his parents, because, having lost hope of ever seeing them again, he's given up trying to find them. His mother and father move closer to the small stoic figure, their expressions turning to joy and disbelief that they've found him and that their search is over. But then their expressions turn to sadness and, it seems, guilt when at first Jim doesn't recognize them.

Then Jim hears his name being called by the voice he wants to remember, and the fog that has numbed his pain begins to lift. He looks up into his mother's face, and wordlessly his expression says "Why?! How could you have lost me? I was a child. I've been looking for you. Have you been looking for me? Are you the voice I've been listening for, the one I have always heard even as my heart began to beat?"

His mother stands in front of him, still saying his name, but we don't hear the sound of her voice. The dialogue is silent because this is their reunion, we only get to watch. Jim looks up at his parents, and he slowly, haltingly, reaches for his mother's cheek and touches it. Then, retreating into the safety of the fog, he pulls his finger back. Refocusing, he takes off her hat and fingers a lock of her hair … pauses, and once more reaches out, this time to touch her lip. All the while Jim's mother and father stand very still as Jim slowly emerges from the pain of his abandonment and allows them to become his parents again. At last, we watch as Jim surrenders. Now he places the palms of his hands on her shoulders and waits for her to respond, and mother and child slowly pull each other into an embrace.

The story ends with Jim's face nestled against his mother's cheek. His eyes open in an expression of disbelief as he feels the softness of his mother, and then they close in a gentle, peaceful repose—Jim is restored to where he rightly belongs. The picture and the music of the lullaby fade out with the scene, the blessing of its lyrics fulfilled.

The scene of Jim's redemption always brings me to tears. Yet my tears are not only joyful tears. I cry out of a personal sense of longing and sadness as well, because my real-life story didn't end like Jim's did—and I'm not alone in saying that—which may be the appeal *Empire of the Sun* has on so many of us.

In 1992, I visited a Romanian hospital annex for children, The place I visited was very different from where Jim's parents found him. The children I met were all HIV-positive and many of them had special needs. No one came to this place to look for these kids because they were orphaned or abandoned to the care of the State. In the story I'm going to share with you, you'll come to know this place as it was officially designated in the Romanian health care system, Post Cura #3. The English translation is "After Care (facility) Number 3". Over time we abbreviated the Romanian name to PC#3.

I went there for two reasons. I was recruited to visit PC#3 as part of a fund-raising trip or I never would have gone there. I had no aspirations of ever visiting Romania and when I asked God "Why there?" He said "There's something there I want you to see". The organization that hosted our trip hoped we would be moved by the experience of being up close to the kids' suffering and inspired by the support our hosts were providing them, then return home and make a large financial contribution. But from what I saw, the kids' suffering was only being marginally alleviated. It was also plain that it would continue and even deepen when our hosts withdrew from PC#3 and went on to other projects. The vision I saw of the kids' future broke my heart, as God had intended it to be broken, a chapter of the story He'd scripted for my life to that point.

The children I met in 1992 had never felt the emotion of longing for a mother. A parent's embrace was an experience they had never had and never would know—and unlike Jim in the relocation center, no one would ever come to look for them. They would end their lives alone in PC#3 or the hospital.

Fiction has its place in my entertainment choices, but I can always put the book down or leave the theater and return to my life. Not so PC#3's children. Their lives and their setting were not fantasy. Unlike a book or a movie script, their suffering was tangible and impossible to ignore.

One evening at a dinner table with old friends, a colleague who is himself a believer said it would be a terrible thing to know the perfect love the Father has for each of us. Some of my fellow believers recoil visibly when I share my friend's transparency. I thought it was courageous of him to be so honest. My friend meant terrible, because as he went on to say, if he were to take that knowledge of God's love and the awareness of it fully into his heart, "I would have to change the way I lived my life. My autonomy would be diminished, fewer of life's decisions would remain under my authority, and my career would be directed by Someone else."

When we look back on our lives, The Author of our stories has made it so that they can't be rewritten. Joys and sorrows are all blended together, each life the product of the choices we've made in response to our circumstances. So, moving on from our pasts, if today we can fully embrace the majesty of God's love for each of us, then as Francis Shaffer has said, "How then shall we live?"

After my first visit to PC#3 in 1992, my choices were made plain to me: *Go home now and try to forget what you've seen. Or wait with Me until my plans for these children are made evident to you. Or don't wait for Me and write your own ending to the story. You choose. You know where I'll be.*

The little boy Jim has a life that's a Hollywood love story, so his story ends as Spielberg has scripted it. For Jim and his parents, their narrow escape from separation and death ends as it should for the genre. For the children being held in PC#3, however, what was to come for them would steal whatever remnants remained of their innocence. I could see it, they could not, and I recoiled from their tears. Then, like all the rest of their visitors, I, too, turned away from them and went home to another life.

What follows are the stories of being sent back to PC#3, leaving behind the life I had authored for myself, and finding joy encouraging some innocents to come out of hiding, to know the love of their Father for the first time. You will hear other stories of impetuous as well as deliberate acts of mercy in this narrative. I will tell you about the others, myself included, who fled the repugnant cruelty of PC#3, but who were drawn by their hearts to not turn away from the hand of a child reaching out to be touched.

That first day in PC#3, I wasn't a fictional parent hoping to find my lost child. I'd been cast as a visitor in a real-time script, unaware that its Author had been writing a story that would start by returning me to a place where I had once been a lost child myself.

HRS

CHAPTER 1

Return to the Fog

*And this is the judgment, that the Light has come into the world,
and people loved the darkness rather than the Light; for their
deeds were evil. For everyone who does evil hates the Light, and
does not come to the Light, so that his deeds will not be exposed.*

—John 3:19-20

September 2, 1992, was the first day we visited PC#3, and it began
as I'd expected it to. I was hopeful, curious, a little afraid, but despite
my emotions being in turmoil, the Spirit had assured me I was ready.

The unexpected came when, rather than following the others
into the building to begin the tour, I stopped involuntarily and
stood frozen, staring down at the threshold of the front door.
Inside the building, there were orphans and abandoned kids
struggling for their lives, trying to understand the cruelty of their
neglect, and I didn't want to experience seeing any more of that
being visited on someone else.

*I knew it would come to this! This is what You wanted me to see? I
know what happens in there! And You want me to join their chaos and
reprise my past through these kids? What happens after that?*

While I waited for an answer, the jet lag, the heat, and the humidity crushed me. There was no letup of the assault on my senses. And the smell ... It was the stench of mold, sewage, and sweat. That wasn't right ... a smell like that? Coming from a pediatric hospital? It was the odor of human waste and too many unwashed people and dirty clothing accumulating in a small place with no ventilation. It came flowing out through the front door on a wave of children's voices and the shouting of caregivers trying to control them. All of this awaited me on the other side of the line, and I drew back from it.

There wasn't anything to stop me: no curtain, no screen, no door—only the threshold of my fear. *I'm afraid, Spirit. There's HIV in there, there's loneliness and chaos, confusion and abuse, tears and screaming. Is there another purpose for being here or no reason at all? What do You want?*

Standing next to me, waiting, my pastor and colleague from home, Greg, brought me back. "What's wrong, Hud? Why've you stopped? This is not like you."

"I don't want to go in there."

"Why?"

"I'm afraid if I go in there it will change my life."

But Greg could not hear what I heard next.

Did I not call you here?

Yes.

Do you trust Me?

Yes, I trust You.

Take a step. Don't be afraid. There's something I want you to see.

When I stepped through the front door, the space around me became quiet and clear. All around me, chaos and noise continued, but I stood observant and protected with sacrificial blood painted over the threshold of my heart, and the evil passed me by. No longer a victim of what I'd lived in my childhood, I had been prepared, made ready to step again into the fog of evil's chaos— only this time as an agent of salt and light, love and mercy.

Yet nothing I'd heard about PC#3 had prepared me for the effect it had on me. Where in the world could you go to pre- condition yourself against the effects of such a terrible place? The smell of the place—along with the sight of sick children clinging to me like fleas, crying for attention, and the unmistakable taste of air trapped in a hot, humid, closed-in building with too many sweating people—was unrelenting. The noise and confusion left me feeling light-headed and nauseated, like the symptoms of hypoxia. I yawned continually, and for several days, I lost my appetite.

Some of the children rushed up and clung to us with inquisitive looks on their faces. I knelt down to reach them. I wanted to know each child. "Who are you? What's your name, where are you from? How old are you?" As I looked into their eyes, some of them stared back from the same vacant, distant fog as Jim in *Empire of the Sun*. Others wanted to touch and be touched, to leave the fog like Jim had when his mother found him. Some eyes flickered with expressions of fear or sadness, others with distrust, and others with evil that challenged my presence. You could smell the evil: it was sharp, acidic, and pungent.

But other eyes "spoke" words, and this I can't explain. I heard: "Are you the one? Do you know what they do to me when you're not here? We've been waiting for you ... will you come back to see me again? The others who came here didn't come back. Do you have a snack for me?" I had spoken those same words to other people in my past, but now they were being repeated to me by these children in their wishful moments.

We began our tour, led by our hosts and PC#3's director,

along with some of her staff. They did their best to try to explain our host organization's program of remediating the effects of the children's neglect, but their chagrin was obvious. They definitely needed the support we were there to raise, but the shame of explaining to strangers how conditions like these could've existed under their watch and been kept secret for years was both awkward and pitiable.

What should you know about this building and the everyday agenda of the children who lived there? The building had been built as a day care center for the children of working mothers. That was during the years before December 1989, when events removed the dictator Nicolae Ceaușescu and his wife, Elena, from absolute power—if that can be said about people with earthly power. Now the building had been taken over and poorly adapted for use as a pediatric residential hospital annex. Designated Post Cura #3, or After Care Center #3, a doctor had chosen the building from the State's inventory of old buildings to house and perform research on a specific cohort of children that she had selected from the hundreds of Romanian children being diagnosed every day with HIV.

In 1990, the mysterious and deadly new virus was emerging, and the international medical research community and pharmaceutical companies were in desperate need of controlled subjects in a controlled environment on whom to perform medical research. Following Ceaușescu's removal, Romania's abandoned children remained in place in their orphanages, the system not yet dismantled. Although the building wasn't suited for residential hospital care, the pediatric wards in the Constanta Infectious Disease Hospital were beyond their capacity to accommodate the new cases. Someone thought PC#3 was adequate to manage the overflow. Thus, a nondescript former day care center became home to fifty-six orphaned or abandoned children, all of whom had been infected with HIV.

Our hosts explained that before the revolution, access to PC#3 was strictly controlled by the doctors in the infectious disease hospital. Furthermore, accurate statistics about the numbers of unwanted children in other places like PC#3 were kept intentionally vague. Why? Because of their shame. In a culture that prided itself on creating citizens who were all productive assets of the State, these kids were nonpersons; they were mistakes the shrinking post-revolutionary budgets could no longer support. They consumed State resources and returned nothing for the investment being made to keep them alive—but their anonymity disappeared when they couldn't be hidden away any longer from the flood of inquisitive Westerners.

These children received everything the State felt they needed for their development from inside the building. They never left. By 1992, when HIV was only just beginning to be understood there, the people responsible for the kids' care thought containment of the virus meant isolation. It was the last thing these emotionally starved kids needed more of. They never got out of PC#3 except to be dragged by the arm, screaming in fear, to the infectious disease hospital for blood draws or infusions. Antiretroviral drugs hadn't reached Romania yet. They may have been on the development drawing boards of the pharmaceutical companies, but it was thought that these kids would never live long enough to receive them or benefit from the application if they did come. In a place that only invested in a life if that life returned something to the State, these kids' lives, as an interest group, were worth nothing to anybody, and there was no central government authority acting as their advocate.

But all that began to change when the people responsible for the kids' medical condition realized that they controlled a cohort of HIV-positive children to whom people in medical research would pay to have access. Now, instead of being liabilities, the kids became a valuable commodity.

As we got to know the staff, I met an unusually engaging and enthusiastic young Romanian woman working as a special needs educator. Her name is Marinela. She taught her kids crafts and simple art projects. Some of the kids she worked with could complete their tasks; others could not. She never lost patience with them.

A few years later, she shared her heart for the children with me in the form of a letter. I asked her if I could include it in my narrative and she said yes. I stored it in my documents under the title "Mari's Prayer." It's highly unusual for a Romanian to author a letter of such uncommon candor and transparency. She said in one page what I've tried to say in five. These are her words, unredacted:

> *I was only 20 years old when I have first entered in an institution for abandoned children, and I remembered that it was one of my saddest days in my life. It was about 1992, the troublous years after the '89 Revolution—years when our first concern was to taste the recent liberty, and each did that in his own style. Some had their own business selling jeans bought from Turkey, listening to their favorite music, or turning on the lights after staying years in dark. Some regret those years when the State gave them houses, regret the empty shop windows, because now they have full shop windows, but they do not have money to buy.*
>
> *I am not one of them. Then, back in 1990s, I understood once again the lie we lived in. I understood that we are not actually the country with wonderful pioneers and smiling faces. I understood that we did not have any reason to thank the party and*

State leaders. I understood that we had a lot to catch up on and that would probably never happen.

The smell was terrible. It could be smelled from the front door, and in the first moment I wanted to turn back and get out. Then I saw the beds—lots of iron beds in rows with the rusty wire that was not completed. Afterward, there were eyes that looked at you, lots of eyes: big and brown eyes, empty and sad eyes. I asked myself what I was doing there, but it was too late to run away. Then I sensed that something or someone pull my jacket, and when I turned I saw those little and fragile hands that were desperately hanging on me, looking for warmth and nurture, love and comfort. I stood there next to the little bed not knowing what to do, thinking that I was so lucky in my life—selfish thoughts that made me feel good in that hostile world.

Innocent children, victims of a regime that did not want them, victims of parents who rejected them, tormented souls.

I left in a hurry, and I said to myself that I will never come back there. But now there are 18 years since then; I left, but I came back again and again. Now the little children are adults. Many of them flew away, some remained with us. They are adults with children's souls; they seem to be stunted in that period when no one wants them and when they stubbornly wanted to live. They refused to grow up and become adults. They are adults with a child's mind. Playing all the time, they do not talk but they hear you. Maybe they do not understand or do not want to let us know that or maybe they want to punish us that we weren't there when they needed us to be next to them.

So many questions arose as our visit came to an end. Tragically lost in the philanthropic agenda was the one question no one wanted to confront truthfully. We wanted to be polite so we avoided asking, "What kind of future will the children have when your program ends and the financial support stops?"

It's a terrible thing to have to say now, but lost in many relief efforts—and it certainly was true about this one—are the children, who were the cause célèbre at the time. The kids were what had drawn visitors to Romania. People came to see them, including our host organization. But inevitably, when our host's two-year collaborative contract with the hospital at PC#3 ended, the children would still be there with less care and less hope than they had had before. People will say, "I wonder whatever happened to those kids?" and then turn to their next distraction. The relief agency will be gone, and the donations with them.

There must be a corollary to the expression "Truth is stranger than fiction," because there are those moments in life when tragic reality confronts us so straightforwardly that we wish it were fiction. But there are also those holy occasions in which the Spirit confronts us, and in a moment of clarity, every event in our lives both terrible and wonderful comes together, and we are stopped dead in our tracks to see the truth. I lived such a moment in 1992.

I was being given a gift in the midst of the madness, just beyond the front door of PC#3, and I didn't see it coming until I stepped over the threshold. There was God as a small child, in a tiny, precious corner of His own heart looking back at me, reaching for my finger. He'd been keeping company with the forgotten least of the least. He wanted me to find Him there over the threshold. But it wasn't until later, as I was drawn back to the place in a kind of morbid fascination, that I realized I was seeing the Creator Himself, vulnerable and suffering, enduring, waiting for someone to act. The first visit utterly broke me. Now, like Mari, I had no choice but to go back to claim the gift He wanted me to see.

Some gift. I could not have imagined what was to come.

CHAPTER 2

The Invitation

But seek first His kingdom and His righteousness,
and all these things will be provided to you.

—Matthew 6:33

Following World War II, there was a period in world history known as the Cold War. From 1948 to 1989, very little was known about everyday life in Romania. Alongside other countries allied with Soviet Russia, it was isolated from the western nations by a wall—the Iron Curtain. Freedom of movement in or out of Romania, except within the Soviet bloc of nations, was a crime.

During those years I wouldn't have known how to characterize the lifestyle of the typical Romanian. With the exception of its seemingly invincible gymnasts who emerged every four years to perform with near-robotic perfection, Romania was another Cold War enigma hidden behind a wall.

The person who thought he needed such a wall was Soviet Premier Joseph Stalin. He divined the need for a barrier to isolate his post-WWII Soviet Union from the prying eyes of his former allies: the US, Britain, and France. In some places, the Iron Curtain was an actual barrier. The Berlin Wall might be one of the best-known examples.

When WWII ended, the Allies imposed their sovereignty over their former adversary, Germany, and divided the city of Berlin into four zones. For purposes of governance, they agreed that the former German capital should be apportioned accordingly. The problem arose when too many residents from the German Democratic Republic, or the Soviet-occupied zone in Berlin, were leaving through Berlin, seeking asylum with the Western occupiers for a more prosperous life—3.6 million in fact. So, the Soviet premier who succeeded Stalin, Nikita Khrushchev, erected another wall in August 1961 to make leaving even more difficult. The Soviets and East Germans were serious about maintaining the integrity of the Berlin Wall—so serious that people attempting to escape over it were shot or arrested on the spot by police guarding the edifice. Even approaching the wall too closely just to look at it invited death, and no one questioned the intent of the East German police.

All of this protective enforcement extended along all the borders of the Soviet bloc, and had the Iron Curtain and the Berlin Wall not eventually come down, the legacy of Romania's unwanted children may still be shrouded in secrecy. But during the Christmas season of 1989, Romania's dictator was overthrown and the Iron Curtain disintegrated virtually overnight. What followed was the period of the Soviet glasnost (openness) and perestroika (listening to its people), and this attitude spilled over into most of the other countries in the former Soviet Union, including Romania.

On the European continent, the Cold War was not a shooting war. To be sure, lives were being lost, but there were no battlefields.

Even so, battles were still brutal—we learned of spy planes being shot down, people being snatched off the streets never to be seen again, and adversarial intelligence agencies spending millions of dollars to disrupt the other agencies' plans. Novels were written about what life for dissidents had been like in Soviet prison camps. Our interest in following these stories reflected the reality of how curious we were about our supposed adversaries. But the underlying message that emerged from our hostilities toward each other was about the futility of it all.

When the Cold War ended, given the opening to explore the unknown culture of our new European neighbors, curious investigative reporters came flooding in, looking for new material to report on, and following the leads of reluctant informers, they began to fan out and explore every cultural and geographical corner of Romania. Videotape began to flow back from these investigators to worldwide news agencies, and images about Romania's forgotten children showed up seemingly every night on our television screens. What at first was thought to be an isolated tragic discovery turned out not to be a one-time anomaly at all. Initial reports were followed by an incomprehensible flood of discoveries of children being kept in indescribable conditions. Many thousands of Romanian children were being warehoused in hundreds of institutions throughout the country.

To make matters worse, it was discovered that HIV was rampant among the pediatric demographic. It was tragic that children were suffering, but HIV? That got people's attention. HIV had been getting more media attention in Western societies in the late 1980s and early 1990s, and it was deadly. Mystery surrounded it because very little was known about the virus's origins. People wondered how it was spread, if its spread could be contained, or if it could even be treated. Statistics generated by the Romanian government and in-country relief agencies were imprecise because the host country's own records were intentionally censored internally. The estimates were that more than 150,000 children—most of them insane from being kept isolated and abused—were being institutionalized, and many of them carried the virus.

Watching the seemingly endless stories of the atrocities, I tried to comprehend the magnitude, the absolute scale of the injustices that so many children suffered. It was illogical, incomprehensible. What kind of persons could mete out such cruelty on the scale we were seeing and call it culturally normal? If one definition of denial is the refusal to acknowledge an unacceptable truth, then no one could perpetrate such an evil and call it in the national interest unless their souls had become numbed to the injustice of it. There had to be a collective national shame that was being rationalized in order to dismiss the practice and look away from it.

I had personal experience of abuse as a child but not anything that could compare to what these kids were being forced to suffer. I could look at the face of a child on the screen and think, *I know how you feel. You want to know: "When will this end? What did I do?"*

But I turned away from the images and dismissed my feelings toward them. What could one man do about a tragedy of this magnitude in a foreign country six thousand miles away? I had left my life of abuse behind, and I thought the only effects that remained with me were the memories of it.

Then, to my surprise, in 1991 I was asked to go to Romania to see some of the children I'd turned away from on the television screen. I was to be part of a fundraising group that would eventually make a gift of funds to our host organization after we visited an orphanage they supported. In a prayer, I asked what my response to the invitation should be. The message in return was, *You're not ready for this yet. You have more work to do.*

The tone of His message wasn't pejorative or judgmental. The Spirit of Truth and I simply had more work to do before the hurt I'd experienced and caused during my turn as a prodigal was healed. No sane person leaves his family. I had. The choices I'd learned to make as a child helped me survive my early years, but now, as an adult, they were self-destructive and harmful, not only to me but to the ones I loved.

I discussed the invitation with my wife, Cynthia, and she agreed to open our home and host a meeting with the others who'd received the same invitation. My caveat was "I won't be attending that meeting, and I'm not going to be going to Romania. While the meeting's going on, I'm going to go into the family room to watch TV." I intended to sit apart since the Spirit had told me that I was not ready to go.

Sometime in early 1992, however, I was finishing five years of very intense work dealing with my past, with the goal of understanding the reasons behind my self-destructive behavior and the consequences of the verbal and physical abuse I'd lived with from early childhood into college. Prior to beginning the work, whenever successes were within reach, I would revert to believing I didn't deserve those successes. I would duck back into the fog to escape failure's pain before I'd even begun to take on the challenge of success. I had trusted the lies of my inadequacy and carried with me a fear of success. I had no fear of failure— I unintentionally welcomed it. I feared success far more because its outcome didn't support my self-image.

I state it this way because it's important for you to know that for most non-resilient people, the fog is an anesthetic. It's a place to escape to. It's an easy fix to go there to avoid the shame of self-doubt. It's no wonder children who grow up learning to escape and become invisible in the fog often go on to find comfort as teens and adults in the more powerful anesthetic effects of alcohol, drugs, sex, food, suicide, or worse, all of them. And to compound the tragedy, they often go on to become repeat abusers themselves, the sins of their fathers revisited upon successive generations until Christ intervenes in a life by invitation and faith.

To recover from the effects of my life of lies, I was shepherded into learning how to choose to seek the voice of the Spirit of Truth. My counselor helped me to learn to use His light to look into my heart to find where the lies resided and replace the effects of them with His love. I had to lose my other life in order to gain full acceptance of the new one (2 Corinthians 5:17).

In a final session, my guide of the past five years said, "You're done now. There's no need to go on."

I told her, "I feel like my heart has been exposed to such an intense spectrum of radiation that I'm of diminished capacity."

"No, Hud," she said. "You're still the same person. You just use fewer words."

Shortly thereafter came another invitation to go to Romania—this time from my pastor, Greg Ogden. He'd been asked to take another group on a second trip to Romania because the first trip hadn't met the host's financial expectations. "And your name keeps coming up in my prayers about who to take. Will you pray about it?" I did—and this time the answer was different.

"You want me to go to Romania? Why Romania? I thought You wanted me to go downtown?"

I do, but after what I've done for you lately, how can you say no to Me?

"I can't. But if I go, what do You want me to do?"

I don't want you to do anything. I just want you to go. There is something I want you to see.

I have a piece of the Berlin Wall on my office credenza. A friend brought it to me. He'd watched while soldiers assigned to guard a border crossing separating East and West Berlin, known as Checkpoint Charlie, stood by and did nothing to stop its destruction. It isn't anything special to look at; it looks like any other ordinary piece of poorly mixed concrete aggregate. But knowing that people may have lost their lives attempting to climb over it, and others who'd built it had used the wall to hide their shameful secrets, it becomes an extraordinary object, not unlike a piece of the moon. Consider this: If a moon rock and a remnant of the Berlin Wall sat next to each other on my credenza, and I didn't explain to you what you were looking at, they wouldn't mean anything to you. But knowing the facts surrounding the disposition of a chunk of concrete, if that piece of the wall were still in place, the stories of the children I'm going to tell you would have never been revealed.

"There is an appointed time for everything … A time to tear down and a time to build up" (Ecclesiastes 3:1,3). Solomon's insight into the timing of our human endeavors is existential, and the nature of our endeavors is revealed to each of us in His time. God has His purposes for us, and it is for Him to know what they are and when to reveal them.

And that's how it was for me as I eventually stood staring at a nondescript building in Constanta, Romania, not knowing what I was about to find. "You crumbled walls and took down governments and dictators; You healed my heart and restored my life; You brought me here to see this?"

Yes. There is something in there I want you to see.

CHAPTER 3

Did You Choose Them or Did They Choose You?

I have seen all the works which have been done under the sun, and behold, all is futility and striving after wind.

—Ecclesiastes 1:14

As we lifted off the ground in Romania and the flight turned toward Switzerland, the feelings I carried with me should have been mounted on the fascia of the Bucharest airport. What every visitor should have read in preparation for transiting the airport and meeting the people of the country in general was: *You're in Romania now, and you're not welcome!*

It was such a stark relief to step out of the heat at the top of the stairway and board the calming, air-conditioned Swiss Air jet with clean, cool blue leather seats and return the smiles of the welcoming Swiss Air cabin attendants. I'd escaped! I had left behind the surly, smirking soldiers sporting camo gear with their AK-47s. Whose idea of hospitality was that in an airport, a place meant to welcome guests to their country?

I'd been freed from an airport with no running water or flushing toilets. Freed from feeling the crunch of broken glass

17

under my feet, staring at bullet holes, stepping over trash, cigarette butts, and feces from the stray dogs wandering around looking for food. Freed from trying to turn a deaf ear to rude customs officials who screamed at me to follow instructions I couldn't understand, demanding money as a bribe to leave their country as I was herded past their desks. I never wanted to see the place again.

My entire tour group was too physically tired and emotionally fatigued to do much talking; most of us were alone in our thoughts or sleeping from exhaustion. I pulled out my trip notes, recalling the first day we visited PC#3. That day our hosts focused our attention on the kids and their daily routines and not on the building or the facilities meant to provide for their care. They wanted to demonstrate their programs to develop the kids' sociability skills and cognitive learning. But if human development also requires clothing, hygiene, food, and nurturing, these kids were barely receiving the basics, and the quality of those basics was not even close to being sufficient.

For example, we were told there were fifty-six kids ages two to five years old, all HIV-positive, under the care of the hospital—many since infancy. The children slept in crowded wards in rows of rusting cribs stacked end-to-end on the first and second floors. Whatever toys or security objects that belonged to them personally were in their beds or under them on the floor. Their hygiene was inadequate due to insufficient numbers of staff to bathe each child daily and keep up with the laundry… and there was no hot water for either. The laundry area consisted of three or four large, galvanized tubs on a concrete floor in a room with a wall-mounted cold-water hose bib.

The bathrooms had been built for a far smaller number of children. The few sinks and toilets that remained didn't work. The others had been taken home by some of the staff. I recall seeing only two enamel tubs for bathing fifty-six kids. The staff had to make do with plastic tubs.

Can you imagine it? Fifty-six children, most not potty-trained, without hot water, washing machines, or dryers? They had one clothesline. It snows in Constanta.

To delay the onset of the virus, HIV patients require hygiene and more than the usual amount of food in a balanced diet. These kids survived on a diet that was mostly a mush of powdered potatoes and formula. There were some canned peas and carrots, containers of applesauce, juice, treats, yogurt, and fruit rolls that were sent over by the hospital when they could spare them. None of it was fresh.

The staff had divided the kids into two groups. One of the groups—about a third of the kids—was referred to as the "upstairs kids." They were the kids who lived on the second floor. These kids experienced a range of profound special needs—from schizophrenia and autism to the effects of fetal drug and alcohol syndrome—along with some not-so-simple physical impairments and psychological and mental issues due to neglect and abuse. The one little boy who stood out was Gheorge. Like most of the upstairs kids, Gheorge couldn't walk or speak. He lay on a foam pad all day and wasn't moved. The staff wrapped his forearms and hands with foam pads, and still his face was contused and bruised from the beatings he gave himself. He'd taught himself the technique as an infant to self-stimulate and prove to himself he was alive. The staff eventually tied his hands together, but then he would wail in frustration until the nurses couldn't stand it any longer. They would untie him and he would start hitting himself again, but he was quiet.

To the kids, the concept of "parent" could only have been an instinct. As infants, most of them had never been held, touched, or interacted with by another human. To the higher-functioning kids who saw me for the first time, I was just another bystander— and a curious-looking one at that. Some of the special needs kids were physically as well as emotionally damaged. Their pain was so great I did not know if they were even aware of me. I watched these kids as they sat and rocked ceaselessly, some banging the backs of their heads against a wall for stimulation, others chewing their fingers to self-stimulate so that their hands became misshapen and gnarled like lepers'. Most did not speak, shielded from the pain of repeated neglect by the coolness of the fog.

The other two-thirds of the kids in residence appeared on the surface to be as normal as any other children. They were referred to as the "downstairs kids," and as with most groups of people there was no ubiquitous norm. Some were as beautiful and bright as any child should be. Mioara was one such five- or six-year-old little girl, but she was one of the few exceptions. Others were not so blessed with a survivor's resilience, even if their abilities significantly distinguished them from the upstairs kids.

The aggressive higher-functioning kids would try for a gift or a hug. We were encouraged by our hosts to not react to them, but I knew no words in Romanian. What was I to do? Turn my back and walk away from one kid, only to find another one in front of me? For that reason alone, I could rationalize ignoring them. There wasn't any way to connect. I'd be gone soon enough, and then the next group of curious onlookers would come to stare at them. The kids didn't expect to see me again, and I knew I'd never be back to see them. I was on a fundraising tour. That effort would have to be enough.

Our host organization paid for special education and speech therapists to help the regular teachers. In time, I learned that relief organizations can attract donations to pay for educational programs with a quantifiable beginning and end. Looking into the future of these kids, I saw a bleak and uncertain set of circumstances. They'd been neglected for so long, they had dead spots in regions of their brains. But if they didn't live long enough to remediate some of the effects of their neglect, what good was a one-year special education program? They needed better food, their own clean beds, clean clothes, a warm house, and love and warmth from another human to instill hope that they'd never known, which could pull them out of their silence. They didn't need short-term education—they needed long-term love and care.

As I watched Romania slide by under the wing, I recalled my moment of clarity at PC#3. My moment contrasts sharply with the fictional Jim's visit by his parents. In *Empire of the Sun*, we see an organized presentation line of smart, disciplined, well-scrubbed, and well-turned-out children following directions, hoping to be found by their parents. That was not what I witnessed at PC#3. Unlike Jim's setting, PC#3 wasn't a compassionate temporary refuge for displaced children being cared for and looked after until their parents arrived to find them. PC#3 was an island in a gulag of State-run holding pens, and the children's stay would end when they died from complications of HIV or other childhood diseases.

Maybe some of the higher-functioning kids would eventually get out to try life on their own, but they would be woefully unequipped to contend with the predators who actively pursued unaccompanied children. I wondered if anyone—our hosts, the kid's caregivers, or anyone in the hospital administration—was allowing for that possibility, multiplied by the number of other children in places throughout the country where children who were HIV-positive were being kept. These children would be trafficked all over the world, and no one would know their real circumstances.

What hopeless futility. PC#3's residents had never known any other life but this one. Alone in their fog, many of them were unable to speak enough to share what they wished for or to convey their loneliness. Even if they could, there was no one there to listen to them. That was my moment of clarity. They had no one to speak for them. These children had no advocate.

CHAPTER 4

I Will Hear His Cry

You shall not oppress any ... orphan. If you oppress him at all, and if he does cry out to Me, I will assuredly hear his cry.

—Exodus 22:22-23

Our hosts had planned our stopover in Zurich as a restorative finish to an emotional experience. Emotional indeed! I couldn't shrug off or dismiss my anger. Or had I confused anger with righteous indignation? I had been up close to a tragedy that was about to be forgotten as foreign investors rushed in to shape Romania's newest and latest reality. The kids and the callous system that dismissed them and their misery would disappear, and with it all of the tragic remnants of a former dictator's cynical view of the value of a human soul.

There was no peace for me, so I walked relentlessly, revisiting Zurich, a city I remembered from when I'd been twenty years old. My underage brother and I bought beers and bratwursts then, and nobody cared. Nobody was there to stop us. Twenty-five years later, I stared at the streets and park benches where we'd sat and drunk our beers; we'd had such freedom then. The sporting goods store where I'd bought a sweater and a knapsack, the bratwurst stands, the hotel where we'd stayed—all of it was still there, unchanged. But I was changed.

As I tried to push away the images of what I'd seen the week before, thoughts of my brother and my childhood reemerged. The hunger, physical abuse, and mistrust of anyone bigger than me were no longer memories. I'd seen it all again the week before. A colleague who went with me that night later said he'd never forget the ferocity of our walk through the city. He told me later he could barely keep up with the pace I was setting. Still, I couldn't walk away from the suffering I'd seen and the terrible question that would not detach itself from their faces.

What if that child in PC#3 were my child? Knowing his longings, could I turn my back to his misery? *He isn't my child— he's someone else's, not mine. And what good can come from my caring if I can't get there? If I'm not there, I wonder, who will take care of him?*

Answer: no one. No one for him or the little girl in the next crib. No one will hold her, entertain her curiosity, bathe her, buy her clothing and toys she likes, read her stories, change her pants, cut her hair, give her sweets or special treats from the kitchen. No one will take her life into their heart as any normal parent would do.

It's easier to dismiss the questions like these when it's someone else's child. Then, in a moment of terrible clarity, the Spirit whispered, "Hud, that is your child, and you, too, are in there with the others. I am in there with them. I am in you, you are in Me. You see and feel what I see. I want you to want their wounds, their hurts, their experiences, and their needs to be known. I want my children returned to Me. I want you to speak for them because you remember …"

Our mother had pulled the Venetian blinds to shut out the

light. It wasn't dark outside; it was a summer afternoon. Closing
the blinds made the light in the room turn yellow. My brother and
I were perhaps nine and seven years old—in a hot, quiet house
on a summer afternoon. We wanted to be outside, playing with
the other kids in the neighborhood, but before closing the
bedroom door, she held up a length of wooden crown molding.
The crown molding was always there. It was her permanent
intrusion into our bedroom, placed on a window ledge in our
room, always there for us to see. "This is here as a reminder. If I
have to use it on you, I will. You boys be quiet until I finish my
nap, or so help me I will use this." The crown molding had been
shattered on us and replaced many times.

She was gone. We stole a glance at each other because we
were hungry. Lunch had been skipped for some infraction. Could
we sneak into the kitchen to steal some bread and not be heard?

We stole out of our room as quietly as we could, but our
movements disturbed her. The door from the hallway burst open.
She grabbed my arm and dragged me to the window ledge, her
anger out of control, her insanity erupting. The blows and her
screaming made me wonder if I would be damaged or killed.
Would the neighbor across the street hear my screaming over
hers and come to stop this? The noise and the beating were like
being under a huge wave. My body was tossed and thrown, and
so, to protect myself, I curled into a ball as small as I could make
myself and waited for her arms to spend themselves, her demons
to be vented out on me.

The noise from her screaming and my cries while her fists
landed on my head and body made a lot of noise. The violence
was confusing and terrifying. To escape, I sent my mind deep
inside to the make-believe womb. Like going into a fog, it was
always cool, and there I became invisible.

Where were my brother, sister, father, or a neighbor? Someone to rescue me, to make her stop, and then comfort me?

I didn't know, and I was beyond caring. Those thoughts and the question "Why?" would come later. For now, I was alone, trying to survive, and hoping I wouldn't be damaged. I was trying to find love in a world where there was only confusion and hate. In that world, it had been better to be alone in the fog, where I had some semblance of control.

As I walked, I did what I usually do when I'm met with a personal failure: I became angry.

How do I walk away from what You're asking? I can't do this! How do I get anybody to step up and help me with these kids? They're six thousand miles away. You want that I should go back and demand the Romanians reverse fifty years of indifference and bad judgment? I'm just another self-important visitor they will ignore and won't remember. I don't know anybody there well enough to ask for help. I have no friends there. I can't understand a word they're saying. I have a life that I've left behind to come here. If I stopped what I'm doing at home to go back, by the time I've gained any traction on the problem the kids will either be moved somewhere else or be dead. How do You expect me to do this?

While I had time before He answered, I fled to the safety of consensus opinion to rationalize my avoidance behavior. What would most people do when faced with a dilemma like this one? Would you disagree with me if I said, "PC#3 is an insurmountable problem way too big for one person to take on. A multinational relief agency with millions of dollars can't turn it around. Their own government can't find the resolve to act humanely. I can't change a government's resolve to repent. What do you expect me to do?" Who could argue with that kind of response?

As I said earlier, my moment of clarity during the visit contrasted sharply with the movie scene of redemption and joy between Jim and his parents. Mine was on a beach near the Black Sea. Our hosts knew how soon the impact of what we'd seen could be dulled by the anesthesia of home's familiar comforts and habits. They wanted the emotional impact of the tragedy we witnessed to remain with us and thus ensure our commitment to organizing a fundraising effort at home. That was the quid pro quo for shepherding us safely on what had admittedly been a potentially hazardous mission. But the first step in cementing our commitment was a manipulated "kumbaya" experience on the beach.

We were asked, "Were your hearts not broken for the tragedy we'd witnessed? But isn't there hope in the kids' futures because of the good works being supported by our organization?"

Was God watching me from a distance in that moment, unmoved? He was not. Did He turn His back to me in Zurich while I complained and turned my back to Him? No, He didn't. He has always been there—my Father, waiting for His prodigal to return. As I struggled with having to accept suffering I couldn't touch, the Spirit whispered, *He suffered while He waited for you, Hud. Can you wait with Me now for your directions?*

Then, as I tried to respond, I heard: *Wait, don't get ahead of Me. You're not going to do this. I am. Wait on me. You sought the kingdom, and I've given you the desires of your heart. Now I will give you what you need to do what I've called you to do. Listen for Me and wait. You're home now.*

While standing with our group on the Black Sea beach, I knelt down, put my forehead in the dirt, and wept.

I'm often asked, "Why did you go there? Aren't there just as many needs in the States? Romania isn't your country."

I'd like to respond with, "If you see needs here, why don't you go to meet them?" but I don't. I usually respond with, "Yes, you're right, there are needs at home. But I was called to go there."

Cynthia later told me when I walked off the plane, "I looked at your face and said to myself, 'My life is about to change.'" I saw nothing different when I looked at my face in the mirror, but she was right about our lives changing. What God had revealed on that first visit had settled something in my heart. A chain of events had begun that changed more lives than just Cynthia's and mine. No one, not even I, could have foretold the roles we would be asked to play in acting out God's purposes.

CHAPTER 5

First, Start a Relationship

... encourage one another in love and good deeds,
not abandoning our own meeting together ...

—Hebrews 10:24-25

There were three planned reasons for my first trip to Romania. The first was to see the work our host organization was doing to relieve the suffering of the orphans and abandoned kids in PC#3. Following our visit, we were to return home and, inspired by their work, raise funds and make a donation in support of the organization that hosted our trip.

The second reason for going was to follow up on the idea of forming a working relationship with a Romanian church. What that meant hadn't crossed my mind, but in general, the idea was to encourage each other to go out from our churches, find people in need, and serve them.

The third reason for going was personal. I wanted to meet the children.

Our hosts scheduled us to meet with community leaders

from government, the hospital, the Orthodox church, and the Holy Trinity Baptist church. Our hosts thought if we Americans encouraged the people we met to realize a more active concern for the needs of the orphans, they might be inspired to do so. Their reactions to our entreaties were predictable. For instance, the leader of the Orthodox priesthood was the Metropolitan Daniel. After listening to us, he became indignant, and he sent us away. His indignity was predictable, the equivalent of any person of high stature being admonished for a deficiency, particularly by foreigners. The chief of pediatric infectious diseases was willing to help us if we'd help her to replace the money she was losing from the shrinking government budgets. Philanthropy and outreach in Romania are practiced as quid pro quo business transactions.

Our last event was to meet the Baptist church's leaders in the basement of their church.

The idea to partner with their church was Greg Ogden's. His intention was to encourage their church and ours to realize the biblical concept of the priesthood of all believers. The idea was that church outreach doesn't originate with the pastors, but it bubbles up from within the church body and doesn't wait for the church leadership to ordain the workers or their work. We would admonish each other—iron sharpens iron, as the Scriptures say (Proverbs 27:17)—to get out from the pews of our sanctuaries and serve those in need in our communities.

In retrospect, for Greg and me to invite this concept of a shared relationship devoted to encouraging them to practice outreach from long distance was naive. In their case, just trying to live without the benefits of the privileges of Party membership meant that they were the underprivileged.

But a few of them had been practicing their faith by

evangelizing outside the walls of their church for years, all the while under the noses of the Communists. If they'd been caught, it meant losing their jobs, imprisonment, or worse. Some church members were police informants, blackmailed by the secret police to report on fellow members' plans and activities. If the church were found to be an organized subversive agent of change, it could have been closed. The risks of being discovered were real.

The basement in the Holy Trinity Baptist church is their fellowship hall. It's where the members and their elder staff hold their meetings and the church's social events. The part of it we met is very small. That night there were three expatriate nurses, three people from our host organization, six church leaders, and five members of our group. In the twenty-eight years I've spent visiting Constanta since that first trip, I've gone back in my imagination to that meeting in the basement of the church many times. I don't know how that many people were able to convene around a table large enough to hold all of us and still fit in such a small room. And I don't know why the elders agreed to meet with us, except perhaps out of courtesy. I think it may have been because of our host's influence, but more than that, it may have been because Baptists are a confident bunch and they don't shy away from a good discussion. They knew what was coming.

Although our host's primary agenda in bringing us to Constanta was for us to raise money for them and to show the local churches that Christians from outside Romania were concerned with their HIV orphan problems—and ask what they, the locals, were going to do about caring for their orphaned children's needs—the second half of our host's agenda was born out of the need to replace the expensive short-term contracts of their expatriate workers. With locals who would work for less than the expatriates, the continuity of our host's programs may have had a better chance of surviving long term. But finding local support from church members, such as volunteers and employees, had found no traction. Romanians' indifference to the problem of thousands of orphaned and abandoned children was understandable, and at the same time, incomprehensible to us Westerners.

The Baptist church's elder staff had heard this message before—there was no sign that we were changing their minds. And so it was that after a lengthy, polite conversation, I found myself watching one of our hosts lose his temper, pound his fist on the desk, and shout, "We've been in these orphanages now for two years and we've been asking you to help and you haven't come. Now where are you and when are you going to come?" There was a pause in the conversation.

Then the pastor of the church spoke. "You know, you're right; we should go. But if you're not going in your own communities in your own country, who are you to come here and tell us to go?"

Even before the meeting began, I felt a trembling in my core, like a shaking, as if I were shivering in the cold. I was afraid that it might be visible, and I remember thinking, "Someone is going to see me!" I tried stifling it. As I listened to the evolving conversation, the shaking intensified. After the pastor had spoken, the room was silent, waiting. I saw the relationship I wanted with the church spiraling down a drain. Literally, I saw a whirlpool of water going down the drain. I thought, *you risk being a fool in front of these people, but you better speak now or this moment will be lost.*

I spoke. I made them an offer of my "self."

"I've been in leadership in my church now for ten years. I've been an elder twice, led the men's fellowship and the board of trustees, and my wife and I have taught Sunday school. In positions of responsibility in our church, I've found it's easier for me to get men to give me a check than their time. They would rather give their money because their time is more valuable to them. So it seems we have a common dilemma. You don't go because in the past when you stuck your noses outside the four walls of your church, you got them cut off by the police. And we don't go because we'd rather give money than our time. I will agree to do this. I will go into the inner city in my community at home and work with poor and homeless people if you will go into the orphanages here. And I will agree to come back here next year to be confessional and accountable to you in my work, if you will do the same with me."

Those were my words, verbatim.

That's when a man sitting two places away from me, who had until that time been speaking Romanian, leaned out over the table, turned, looked directly at me, and said in perfect English, "I agree with you. That is the basis upon which I can form a relationship."

As I leaned out to look back at him, I thought to myself, *Why you wily——! All this time you've been speaking Romanian, going through an interpreter, and now you speak in English?* I can't forget his blue eyes looking at my expression, reading my thoughts perfectly, and winking at me.

There were a few people in the basement room that night whose lives were redirected from that moment on, and so were the lives of many more people who weren't there.

CHAPTER 6

Those Who Return Your Peace Will Help You

And whoever does not receive you nor listen to your words, as you
leave that house or city, shake the dust off your feet.

—Matthew 10:14

Like most married couples with young families, Cynthia and I
rarely had time for each other in the mornings back in the early
'90s. While the kids were still at home, there wasn't time to sit and
talk. But after that first trip to Romania, she'd seen something in
my countenance she didn't recognize, and for the following week,
after the kids had left for school and the house was quiet, her gift
to me was her listening ear and her patience. We sat together
while I spun out the stories of what I'd seen. I read from my trip
notes, taking the narrative a day at a time, because one day's trip
experiences were about all I could manage while staying calm and
keeping my concentration.

I described what I'd seen of the remnants of the Ceaușescu
era and the impact its anthropology had had on me. But Romania
stood in such stark contrast with our own lives, it wasn't until she

37

went with me that the impressions she had gathered from me became her own. Until then, my words were mere adjectives and my newfound countenance inscrutable.

With my first trip to PC#3, I'd stepped back into the fog. With me came a peace, and with the clarity that came with it, I was able to see and experience a terrible sadness. Now at home, my imagination whirled, and it wouldn't let me rest. Looking for any excuse to get back there, I was driven to get under the surface of the façade I'd been allowed to see and become a part of the sadness. Until that trip, other pursuits had drawn my attention. They didn't matter now. I had to go back there and find a way to get my foot in the door. I'd find a way to get back to Constanta—and once I was there, I'd work the angles and get into PC#3.

So what was it that settled my confusion? I wanted to look into the children's eyes again, to bring His peace with me—and this time, draw them to myself. I wanted to tell each one how much I loved them and push back their grief.

While we were in-country, we'd been told by our hosts that their biggest problem was not persuading people to help relieve the needs of the children still being kept in the institutions. It was persuading the people themselves to come to help our host perform the work. "We have the money, but not the human resources, trained or not. We need people willing to serve." Motivated by what I'd seen and heard, I arranged an interview with the development office of our host organization to see if they would support me in a Romanian project. I asked them if they would allow me to take over the program in PC#3. I would go back to Romania, start a new project, and manage it if they would help me with financial support and guidance.

I saw two people that day. The first man let me down slowly by sharing his frustration with being employed by our host as only a consultant. If not as a project author and manager per se, he said, then the next best thing for him to do was perform the necessary role of finding funds to support the organization's work in former Soviet bloc and developing countries. "As a consultant," he said, "I never get to finish a job. I just find the money. I'd like to go myself, because in my role here I never get to see the work completed. It's frustrating." In my second interview, the young woman said: "You've had an emotional experience. I hear you have a big house. Why don't you help us by having cocktail parties and do fundraising receptions for new donors?"

Flying back to the Bay area, I had time to reflect on what I'd learned. Donated money supports its friends, but actual relief work should wisely be closed to people with good intentions but no credentials. My interviewers were correct. I wasn't an employee of an organization friendly to them, nor did I have any experience working in foreign relief projects or with special needs children with HIV.

But wasn't willingness what they said they needed most? Hadn't they said their greatest need in Romania was for people willing to help? Instead I was supposed to give cocktail parties for Jesus? That comment lit a fire. She was right. I'd had an emotional experience. After experiencing it, I wanted a principal's role, not a component on an organization chart. If I stayed in the US, contact with PC#3 and the hoped-for relationship with the church would be forgotten as another well-intentioned conversation with a curious visitor.

I accepted the challenge. If that avenue wasn't open, I'd try building a relationship with the Baptist church. That could take time, too, but at least I'd be in-country pursuing them—and by being there, I might find a way to get my foot in the front door of PC#3. With no understanding of where it would take me, I set my mind on becoming a part of those children's lives.

But after I'd been home several weeks, nothing was stirring. I went to my traveling companion and pastor, Greg. I said if the two of us were serious about having a relationship with the Baptist church, some of their people were going to have to come here to California and spend some time with us. We had gone there—maybe they'd come to see us if we invited them.

Greg asked me what I had in mind. I proposed approaching their pastor with an invitation to come and speak in our church. We would ask him to bring some of the elders we met that night in the basement. If a relationship was to be built, we needed the pastor and the laymen—especially the man with the blue eyes.

Fifty years of Stalinist ideology remained embedded in Romania's DNA, and the Baptists had a lot to say about its effect on the human soul. They had lived with persecution because of their beliefs. I wanted to hear more stories of practicing their faith in Ceauşescu's Romania.

Ceauşescu had plagiarized Stalin's pragmatic theology for Romania, and nonconformity could land people in prison. A citizen had no personal choices in life except a spouse. The individual was an asset of the State. For the State to succeed in the vision of the great leader, every person had a role to play assigned by the State. Ceauşescu provided everything needed to survive and perform each role as a citizen, including training and education, the career that followed, the recreational facilities, the goods and services, etc. All of it came from the State and out of the generosity of the great leader himself. He shared his treasure with individuals, but each according to his own need.

Naturally, it followed that since every good thing came from Ceauşescu—who would need a God? If you believed in a triune God as the Giver of life, and that each life had a soul, and that each soul would have an eternal destination when the meaningless suffering imposed on it by a despotic fool was over, you and the others like you were a threat to the despot's control.

The people I met in the Romanian church had a faith in a triune God. I believed their stories would appeal to the members of our church. In 1993, my generation of "Baby Boomers" had grown up during the Cold War. If our Romanian brothers accepted an invitation to share their lives in a series of home meetings, I thought others would want to come to those meetings to hear their stories.

Make no mistake though—having been in the world but not of it, these men had earned and deserved their dignity. I suspected that given their discernment, our invitation couldn't come off looking like some kind of ecumenical sideshow being promoted by curiosity seekers. They would stay in our homes while they were with us, and when they weren't speaking at night, during the day we would have some fun touring with them to show them what our side of "the Wall" looked like.

They would naturally be curious about us. They might insist on knowing: "Who are you? What do you believe? How do you live your faith?" Given their life experience, questions like these were to be expected. Only the pastor had been outside Romania to visit Europe. None of the people I hoped would come, including the pastor, had seen the United States. Whatever they knew about us came to them over Radio Free Europe or the BBC, from listening on illegal radios to broadcasts that the Romanian government tried to block.

Before and after the December 1989 revolution, people from the West didn't take cruises on the Danube River or the Black Sea to explore "exotic and mysterious" Constanta. There wasn't a tourist industry in Eastern Europe before the Iron Curtain came down. Hotels were run by the secret police to house and keep track of foreign diplomats and trade missions or for visiting athletic teams. Staying in a friend's home when they traveled was something the Romanians were accustomed to. Cynthia and I thought if we offered ourselves as friends and fellow believers, they might come. We'd have coffee in the morning, take walks together, go to the city, see Monterrey, have dinner together, and have talks in a series of home meetings where they would tell their stories. It might be a start to something more.

Having a relationship with a church in Romania in 1993 was an idealistic notion. What end would come from this? My conclusion was that these men had been made available to me, and it was my call to offer them our peace and to see if that peace was returned. If they chose not to accept our offer of fellowship, so be it. But if I didn't ask, the ready opportunity of getting back to PC#3 would be lost.

CHAPTER 7

Courtship with Strangers

---

*Grace, mercy, and peace will be with us, from God the Father
and from Jesus Christ, the Son of the Father, in truth and love.*

—2 John 1:3

Today, if couples choose to, technology has made it possible to
"meet" someone and you never have to leave home. We meet in
"chat rooms," virtual rooms that appear on the screen of your
computer or smart phone, which for some removes the awkward
sense of being physically present with someone new. Today's
couples don't casually hit on each other like we did. Nowadays, it's
common to "click" on each other to begin a relationship. Click on
the medium of your choice 24/7, 365 days a year, at any time of
the day or night—and in real time, you can meet somebody or send
a message to a friend, a business acquaintance, or a family member
anywhere in the world. But I couldn't do that in 1993. To reach the
pastor and not leave the US, I had to make a telephone call.

In 1993, 99 percent of the world's peoples communicated
through two-way telecommunications networks. Only 1 percent of

the information being exchanged between people was flowing via the internet. By 2000, internet communications rose to 51 percent; by 2007, 97 percent. But from 1992 to 2007, those numbers didn't apply to Romania. Had I wanted to use the internet to initiate a conversation, I would've had to wait six more years. Fiber optic cable wasn't available in Romania until 1998, and only then to those with access to "special friends." Until the year 2000, computers were an expensive and superfluous dream for Romanians.

Just make a telephone call to Romania and invite them to come. It sounded simple enough—but not in 1993. It could take hours a day of incessant redialing, because the Romanian telephone system hadn't been upgraded to manage the volume of calls coming from inside the country and at the same time from outside the country. In-country, every citizen's phone calls went through the post office telephone exchanges, where they were randomly censored by government listeners. Ceauşescu simply had not anticipated the need to invest in a communications infrastructure that could keep up with calls coming from outside the country. Any form of interaction with people from outside had been illegal, punishable by imprisonment. After all, to Ceauşescu's way of thinking, if telephone communications with people from other countries became the norm, it would've meant Ceauşescu was no longer in power, which to him was inconceivable.

A written invitation wasn't a possibility either. Before leaving for home, I asked my new Romanian friends for their mailing addresses, but they advised us not to bother. Ceauşescu might be gone, but some things still had not changed. They said a letter from the West might still prompt the authorities to watch them. Letters with Western postmarks were routinely opened for censoring, the letters themselves discarded and any contents with value pilfered. The postal workers were usually party members, and old workplace standards for suitable materials to be admitted into the country were still in place. Extra-postal services such as FedEx, DHL, or UPS were still far into the future for Romania.

So to reach the pastor, it had to be a phone call. Romania is ten hours ahead of us. I timed the call to reach him at home and kept dialing. After a few attempts, I was shocked when he answered. I'm speculating, but it may have been that my call got through because of his status as a "person to be watched." He had been active in the Baptist Union, protesting government restrictions on their faith in methods that were not passive-aggressive. He once shared with me that he'd unknowingly proselytized the chief of the Constanta secret police section on the beach. He said the man listened quietly and expressed an interest in wanting to know more, but then he was forced to disclose his identity to my friend because he was being watched by his cohorts. "I'm always watched," the man said, "and we're being watched now. So, I'm going to have to raise hell and throw you off the beach. But it's for my safety as well as yours."

As foreign investments began to grow, however, Westerners new to the country expressed their resentment at having their calls monitored. (Not that it mattered to the government.) I found many of my calls in the early years were taped as well. More than once during my phone calls, the phone unexpectedly clicked off and went dead. The first time it happened, when we reconnected, I asked my friend and ministry partner Adrian (also called Adi) what had happened. "Short tape" was his terse comment.

When the pastor and I connected, I offered my invitation and asked him to bring two other people of his choosing. From my memory of the basement meeting, I knew who I hoped would come. As their leader with English skills, the pastor was the obvious first choice. I remembered another man from that meeting. He was quiet and calm with prematurely white hair. He was thoughtful, and when he did speak, it was to direct a few questions to his own people. He looked at me impassively, his gaze hinting curiosity, and I don't remember him saying anything to us. I wanted him to. But the one I wanted most was the man who had winked at me. Later I'd learn that his name was Adi, but then, I knew neither names nor statuses in the church.

The pastor said he would talk to his people. When the elders held their weekly meeting, one of the issues they deliberated was whether they should accept the invitation to come to Saratoga, California. For so many people in the world, California was a magical place: home of the Beach Boys, Hollywood, Silicon Valley, San Francisco, the Golden Gate Bridge, Disneyland, the Pacific Ocean, orange trees, deserts, and snowy mountains.

The elders debated sending three men from Romania to California to visit with some relative strangers. It was an expensive and discretionary wager on an uncertain outcome. But those who are drawn to each other and called by the Spirit will succeed in their work, even if in the beginning they cannot fathom the reasons why. The hand of God is most likely the best answer. For those of us bound with a third cord (Ecclesiastes 4:12), our Father had something in mind.

The pastor has been characterized by his people as a "cricket." Small, extroverted, and very bright, he had an interest in almost everything and everyone he met. He is a gifted teacher and pastor, and he connects quickly with an audience. He was intrigued by this chance to come to the West to see the people who'd been broadcasting forbidden radio messages to him over the Iron Curtain. Their pastor was curious, and he thought they should go. The staff of the church agreed with him, and they blessed his desire to come to California.

CHAPTER 8

Coming to America

... do not go to your brother's house on the day of your disaster;
Better is a neighbor who is near than a brother far away.

—Proverbs 27:10

Adi was a formidable personality. Whether he was being peaceful and loving, angry and irascible, contemplative, or speaking out to teach or correct, he was convicted and clear about what he thought. Talk to people who knew him—he was never remembered for having disappeared into a crowd. Even when he was sitting quietly, observing, or worshipping, you knew he was there because people expected him to speak up in affirmation or objection to whatever was being discussed or preached. And yet despite his strenuous objections to visiting us in California, the senior pastor felt that if anyone should be included in a delegation from their church, it should be Adi. In 1993, Adi and two others were chosen by the elders of the Holy Trinity Baptist Church to go to California to share with the people of Saratoga Federated Church the experience of living out their faith in Romania under the oppression of Nicolae Ceaușescu.

45

US Immigration required visitors to go through the visa application process in person at the US embassy in Bucharest. This process was pejorative and, for me, shameful and embarrassing. Some of my Romanian friends would rather apply for a visa through the lottery program and take the chances of waiting for their number to come up, if ever, than submit themselves to the abuse experienced at our embassy. US embassy staff disdained the process of screening to such a degree that they employed Romanians to screen the applicants.

Our guests, however, were accustomed to these kinds of abuses from other Romanians; they'd lived with the demeanors of overbearing officials with their hands out and were adept at playing the game of point-counterpoint. That day at the embassy, they put on their thick skins and received permission to come to California.

Like all the national highways in post-revolutionary Romania, the original road connecting Constanta to Bucharest was only two lanes. To drive in Romania, their pastor once said, "You need four things: good cars, good roads, good drivers, and God's grace. But we only have one of them: God's grace." The day Adi drove them to Bucharest to get their visas, one of the men had to get out of the car and walk part of the way to keep Adi from driving off the road. The fog near the Danube River bridge was so thick, the road was invisible.

When the day they were to leave finally came, the pastor managed to get a call through to me to let me know they had been stopped at the airport and forbidden to board the plane. They had passports, visas to the US, recorded affidavits of support from me, and round-trip tickets to fly. But to change planes in Frankfurt, the Germans required a transit visa. Lufthansa neglected to tell them the visa was required, and they were stopped at the gate in

Bucharest. They could obtain transit visas through the airline, but their arrival in the US was postponed for ten days.

But all the delays and aggravations were worth it. News passed about these men and the stories they were telling by word of mouth, and over eight nights in people's homes, we were surprised by the number of people who came to hear them speak. They told of being forced to sign statements denying God's existence if they wanted to be given the best jobs after graduation from a university—jobs with the best benefits—to be able to shop in the best stores that provided access to Western goods unavailable to the regular citizens, and to have their children be given access to the best health care and the best schools. Membership in the Party was a prerequisite to these privileges. Only the brightest and best students were accepted into the universities, and of that group only the best were recruited by the Communists upon graduating. They were considered an asset of the State, belonging to the State for service to the State, using their natural gifts and the skills they'd acquired while achieving their degrees.

They told us about the disappearances of people who'd antagonized the State by speaking or teaching on disapproved topics; of cars running up on sidewalks and snatching, killing, or injuring people; of informants in the workplace, schools, and in their churches. The pastor told us that before the revolution, after lengthy and tortured debate among themselves, the leaders of the Baptist Union signed a letter telling the dictator Ceauşescu that he should stop saying that he was God on the nightly State television broadcasts. The Baptist Union's petition to Ceauşescu carried with it considerable personal risk. They feared the consequences to their churches and their families. In fact, his wife told him when he got home from the congress, "That's good, I'm proud of you.

But I want you to walk or drive the kids to school yourself for the next few weeks just to avoid 'accidents' occurring."

Two weeks after submitting their petition to the dictator, Ceaușescu was overthrown and executed during the December 1989 revolution. The pastor went on to say to us in our home meetings that he wished they'd signed the petition a lot earlier.

What emerged from our home meetings, and the question-and-answer sessions that followed, added to what we were already learning about our friends' lives from the numerous intimate and lively conversations around our kitchen table. These men were proud but modest, mature people. They described the discrimination they'd experienced for the choices they'd made in a humble, often humorous and gracious manner, and with great dignity. Nothing about their testimonies was maudlin; they weren't looking for sympathy from us. At some level, they were looking for an opportunity to challenge us. How we reacted to that challenge was just as important to them as was my interest in knowing what was going to be important to them in their next life, post-Ceaușescu.

They described what life was like as a minority faith, practicing their call to risk evangelizing under a repressive political regime that only recognized the legality of the Eastern Orthodox faith. The Orthodox Church was the church of the government and the majority of the population. Approximately 97 percent of the Romanian population practices the Eastern Orthodox faith. It is an institution sanctioned by the government, and the Orthodox church looked after its interests with the government's protection. The Orthodox priests viewed the evangelical church as a threat to their franchise over the gathering of fees. Priests are paid by the celebrants to bless christenings, marriages, and funeral services. Tithing to support the institution of the church isn't a part of their orthodoxy. You may see why other churches' efforts to evangelize are seen as a threat to the fee structure of the Orthodox church.

Juxtapose into this last paragraph Christ's confronting the practices of the temple priests while witnessing His New Covenant, and you may gain a sense of the danger to the State the Orthodox leaders tried to convey to Ceauşescu and why he sided with them.

In these meetings and conversations lie the beginning of my understanding of the likelihood of reaching the kids in PC#3 through the efforts of our friends, the local Romanian church. Our new friends' most pointed questions to us were, "Given the freedom and resources that you have in your country, why haven't you sacrificed to evangelize more?" Our questions directed toward them were, "Why haven't you volunteered to reach the injustices of your own community?" Their questions, like ours, were directed at defining our different priorities. Americans volunteer in their communities and the world as an expression of their empathy for the least of the least, arising out of our faith. We don't feel threatened in the least if our orthodoxy is in the minority. Volunteer efforts common to our culture don't exist in Romania. Their lives belonged to the State in the years before the revolution in 1989. They were to perform for the State in return for the investment the State made in them. If you couldn't, you were left behind. That mindset exists here, too, to some degree. We, too, look to the government to resolve matters of injustice to the poor and disenfranchised—but not to the same degree as the Romanians. It was not a better culture, not a worse one; but if PC#3's kids' futures were to be altered, I had to learn by degrees that our own ethnocentricity wasn't going to inspire Romanian volunteerism.

A matching process was taking place—a courtship to assess

mutual intent—and it took place mainly between Adi and me. Adi was a nationalist hoping to see his country emerge from its shame. He later tired of that ambition, but in my home as a visitor, he saw an opportunity in me just as I saw one in him.

If resources and help were coming, he wanted a role in that future. I saw someone who would act. Neither of us knew how or on what level, but that is the nature of falling in love. We would find out about each other under duress. That's what happened as God intended it to, because for what was to come, love was the essential prerequisite. It became the foundation for our relationship.

Over the years, other visitors from the US have come to Constanta asking for a relationship. Listening to them, I realized how naïve their entreaties were, just as mine had been. As it turned out, despite what Adi said later—"Hud, there is no relationship between our two churches, the relationship is between you and me"—a relationship between the churches did emerge. It was because our works in Constanta were so out of step with the norm in Romania, and we came back so often, that in time our relationship received recognition by our respective churches. But for now, when he left our home to return to his own, I just wanted to see him again.

For those who are listening to the Spirit, God wisely reveals His purposes by degree. Other times He's more direct. People also reveal their thoughts with the expectation of an outcome directed toward their interests, but we're not always trustworthy. To some degree, that practice is the essence of intelligence work. However, as the relationship between two strong personalities developed, I was never sure which of us was handling the other. Was Adi the case worker, or was I? As it turned out, God was handling us both.

CHAPTER 9

Find the Rules and Break Them

In all labor there is profit, but mere talk leads only to poverty.

—Proverbs 14:23

Before they left, we were invited to revisit Romania as their guests, and we accepted. From that first event some had called "our chance meeting" in the basement of their church, a remarkable thing had happened. A relationship had begun to emerge, all the more remarkable because it was being made possible by the one person who had been dead set against it from the beginning. Adi, who had been all for a relationship with me in the basement of their church, had dug in his heels at the idea of going to California—but now he was offering us his home as a place to stay.

I didn't know him that well yet, but I thought his reluctance to visit us in the US was because he was very sensitive to the amount of criticism and ridicule being directed at his country for its treatment of its abandoned children. A second reason may have been because of the history of abuse Romania had suffered from the invasions of other stronger nation-states, which had eclipsed Romania's sovereignty while pillaging her resources. The first invaders were the Romans, then the Ottomans, followed by the Hapsburgs, the Nazis, and finally by the occupying Russian army after WWII. Then there were their own dictators, Gheorghe Gheorghiu-Dej and Nicolae Ceaușescu, who under the guise of benevolent nationalism stole from them just as all the others had. And now there was this current plague, the hordes of curious Westerners speaking out about one of the worst remnants of their abuse under the Communists—the atrocities in the orphanages.

Adi was very private about his feelings for the children—all Romanians were—but not about politics per se. He could be very outspoken about those competing ideas. Still, he was sensitive, even angry, about what he felt were the self-inflicted wounds his country had suffered over the course of their history. He felt Romania's people had brought them on themselves. They hadn't had a sufficient sense of unity and character to accept the idea that it was in their national interest to resist foreign occupiers. I would even say he was embarrassed to have to discuss their history, except for that of the mountain people.

The mountain people were those fierce characters who lived in the Carpathian Mountains who had never been subdued by any occupying force. They survived the invasions and resisted political impositions, protected by their defensible mountain topography while waiting for the invaders to be weakened by the cold and the snow. Adi himself was from the mountainous regions. He had grown up near the Russian border.

Let me explain the appeal of Ceaușescu because it's germane to understanding the Romanian history of confronting injustice—as well as Adi's concerns about our relationship in the beginning. Before Gheorghe Gheorgiu-Dej, the first Communist dictator after WWII, Romanians had suffered the indignity of foreign occupations as they always had. Gheorghiu-Dej and later

Ceauşescu, easily fit Romania into the Soviet bloc of nations, and the Russians allowed them to stay in power because they were Communist. But they gradually elevated Romania's sovereignty above the other members of the bloc of Soviet states and united the country politically by defying the Russians—particularly in their Cold War policy of isolationism. The Romanians loved him for it and overlooked his personal excesses because he provided stability and identity after the chaos brought on them by the Second World War, not unlike a certain German leader who stabilized his country after the chaos of another world war.

But as he gained strength, his other actions were not quite so beneficial to the Romanian people. Ceauşescu thumbed his nose at Russia by making strong overtures to the NATO partners. He paid off foreign debt by industrializing the economy, but he eradicated Romania's grain production, nationalizing the lands of the class of people who produced it. That was a shame because the sale of Romania's grain production had made her the breadbasket of Europe and a world economic power. Instead of embracing that, Ceauşescu centralized the economy so that very little of the country's GDP trickled down to the population, even as he built his own vision of a nation-state. With that came socialism, which meant everybody had a job and everything in the infrastructure worked, but he kept it all in place with fear and intimidation while his people starved.

Yet they had something now they'd never experienced before: they were united by a strong leader who gave them a sense of national identity while the indignities that lay below the surface were forgiven. The people learned it was better—and infinitely safer—to give an oblique glance at the political prisoners who defied him and the children in institutions who had been stolen from their families than to defy Ceauşescu.

In later years at dinners with my closest Romanian friends, I was told more than once, "You're not going to like what we're about to tell you, but you're our brother and we want you to know our feelings." I knew what was coming next. "Under Communism things were better for us. We all had jobs and money to spend. There wasn't anything to buy, but everything in the country worked. Now nothing works, everything is broken, and there are lots of things to buy but we don't have money to buy them. Under Communism we knew who was corrupt. Now everyone is corrupt. People with all the money don't pay taxes."

What I wanted to say in response was: "Yes, but now you're only thinking of yourselves again. How can you rationalize a system that accepted euthanizing thousands of unwanted children as normal? And now we're left with hundreds [no one knows the real number] of HIV-positive children being trafficked and sent all over the world."

But I didn't because I knew this expression of their frustration with their new-normal-post-Ceauşescu social democracy was the answer to my question. Where would I find anybody to step forward in Romania to lead a turnaround of PC#3? People with the time and desire to step into the suffering were too few because they needed financial support, which left only those from the West. As long as Romanians were able to overlook the rot of the old regime and reminisce about it, they would not help unless someone led them and paid them for it.

Now you know why I was trying to sort out Adi's intentions. Why his change of heart? What new vision of the future did he see that may or may not have coincided with mine? I was beginning to learn that Adi's view of things could change very quickly. When he was invited to visit America to see us, he would say, "Nothing will come from this, it's a waste of time. To them we're just a curiosity." He didn't want to be disappointed again. But he may have finally seen my intentions, the portent of things to come. Perhaps he knew before I did where a source of support would come from.

Consider for a moment that in 1993, Romania wasn't getting much play by the travel industry as a vacation getaway. In fact, when we mentioned to our friends in passing that we were about to go to Constanta, it raised some eyebrows. We were asked: "Romania? Why are you going to Romania? What're you going to do there? That was that guy Ceauşescu's country, isn't it? Wasn't he killed? Where is Romania? Isn't that where they found all those kids? Oh, that should be interesting."

And so hour by hour as we traveled farther and farther away from California, the appearances and the demeanor of the people we met changed. On the flight from San Francisco to New York, our mannerisms and appearance weren't that different from the other passengers. From New York to Zurich, our appearance was less like the others, and a few of the passengers were not as patient boarding or disembarking the airplane. From Zurich to Bucharest, the behavior of some of the passengers was akin to an open-air market with too little food to buy. After we boarded the airplane, the Swiss cabin attendants had stepped in to slow the pushing and shoving and settle arguments over disputed seats. When the airplane began its final approach and some of the passengers got up out of their seats and raced the others to the front of the cabin in order to be the first to get off in Bucharest, the Swiss cabin attendants became apoplectic.

Smoking was still permitted on airplanes then. When we

arrived in Bucharest, we'd been up twenty-seven hours, and we still had to get through customs, followed by a four- or five-hour drive to Constanta with Adi. We hadn't yet learned the importance of stopping over in Zurich to rest for one or two nights. On later trips, we overnighted in Switzerland to walk off the jet lag and wash off the smoke and airplane grit that settles on you from just sitting in a coach seat, unable to lie down for a day and a night.

Before we traveled, I tried to prepare Cynthia for what was to come in Bucharest. I explained how the customs people at the Bucharest Airport relished bullying new arrivals. The government didn't closely watch the unsanctioned practice of collecting cash from noncitizens that they called a "visa tax." I told Cynthia, "They'll ask you for $34.00. That's official practice, but the amount will vary depending on how effective they are at intimidating you. Don't lose your cool. After they collect the money, the official will give you half of a little paper receipt. Use this paper clip I'm giving you to attach the half they return to you inside your passport because you're required to present it on the way out of the country. Unless you present it, they'll grill you and threaten you with questioning by the police because without the paper you won't be able to prove you've entered the country legally. They are trained to track every foreigner who's entered the country, and they still employ the old gatekeeper system of bribery."

At the airport, we and our box of gifts and luggage were targets for the customs officials. They were brutish and rude. They demanded we pay tariffs for our "imported goods" or we would have to surrender our box of gifts to customs. Despite my warnings, Cynthia was not prepared, and there was nothing I could do to shield her from the torrent of abuse. In return, I was forced to be loud and abusive myself until higher officials with better language skills stepped in and heard my threat to file complaints at the US embassy. And all this took place before we left the baggage claim area. This was not going well.

Adi met us outside baggage claim, and we finally felt safe because he knew the language.

This is also when Cynthia experienced firsthand how we in the West are different from those in the East. I'm not easily intimidated, but both Cynthia and I found the dangers on the road to Constanta frightening. Adi's joked with us over the years that Romanian roads are "a true democracy," and he's right. Every possible moving object in Romania, animate or inanimate—be it one animal, herds of animals, flocks, a cart, a truck, a car, or a pedestrian—exist on the highway from Bucharest to Constanta, moving in different directions at different speeds. The protocol for traffic is self-interest and disorder, just like the procedure for getting on or off the airplane.

For example, the accepted maneuver for passing other cars or trucks is to play "chicken" with the oncoming traffic and head straight for it. Room to pass? Who needs it? Those approaching from the opposite direction are expected to slow down and allow you to ease back into the lane of the cars you've passed, if the cars you've passed slow down enough to create a space for you to move back in among them. Drivers traveling at breakneck speeds have to cooperate in a deadly ballet and with split-second timing to avoid an accident. It's really unnerving. To find peace I adopted a fatalistic attitude of acceptance.

Cynthia later wrote:

> *To host three elders from a Christian church in Romania had been for Hud and me an amazing experience. We felt a common bond with these fellow believers to whom Christ's salvation is everything. Their faith walk has traditionally been through preaching and teaching. They found our church different than*

they'd expected, especially in terms of its global and local outreach
efforts. During their visit, God had begun laying the groundwork
for what He wanted, but even so, I wasn't prepared for the rigors
of the trip and all that I was about to encounter.

After two days, we were finally there in front of Adi's block of
flats and carrying our luggage and the gift boxes up the three
flights of stairs to his apartment. His apartment was in an old,
musty, dark building. There may be hundreds of people living in
buildings like these, but they are quiet and still. No noise comes
from the neighbors, only the smells of frying meats, onions, and
peppers. The stairways and landings are dark, so you push a switch
on a landing and the lights will come on for maybe ten or twenty
seconds. Sometimes the switches didn't work if the neighbors had
not fully funded the block association dues. I learned to memorize
the number of steps on each landing to be safe and not trip in the
pitch dark. Nine steps up, turn right, and then eight more to reach
the next level. It's the same in each block of flats built in Romania
during a certain period. I memorized the floors and doors of my
friends' flats to avoid intruding on a stranger. Adi's was on the
third-floor—the first door to the left at the top of the stairs.

But then came the most precious moment. When we opened
the door, warmth, hospitality, love, and good smells poured out
over us. Like the passing through the wardrobe door to Narnia,
we had crossed into another world. In Adi's family, there was
peace, culture, order, politeness, and humor.

After introductions in English and a warm, filling dinner, they
put us to bed, exhausted, in the main bedroom. And for the
remainder of our stay, and each successive visit, they slept on
hard couches in the living room, and we slept in their bedroom.
They insisted on this arrangement.

Adi's flat was like a thousand other flats, all of them the same size and the same floor plan. The kitchen was tiny: a single sink and a tiny propane stove and oven with no thermostat. (Yet the food they prepare is exquisite, hearty, and tastes so good!) That's how Romania treated its people and its orphaned children. The State doesn't recognize the non-elites beyond their designated function to the State. The flat had been given to Adi and his wife after an eminent domain proceeding to make room for a government office building took their home.

Early in their marriage, they had bought a house for their new family near the sea. It had a yard and a garden where the breezes from the ocean would cool them in the hot, humid summer months. It had an arbor over the patio and an outdoor brick oven, like a pizza oven, for cooking and grilling. It was one of the better neighborhoods near the Black Sea. A government official had knocked on his door one evening to tell Adi that the State would take the house and level it like it had thousands of other homes in hundreds of other neighborhoods. Many thousands of Romanian families had had more than their homes taken from them in similar proceedings. Personal dignity? What good was dignity to a human asset of the State?

Bitterness was warranted by the Romanians for so many past indignities, and Adi had experienced his share of them. The difference between Adi and most of the others was that he responded by acting out proactively—if anything, he defied them. "Find the rules and break them" was a favorite expression of his—to further God's kingdom. Only privately would he admit he enjoyed thumbing his nose at the authorities.

For instance, the Communists limited the number of divinity students to be admitted to university. So, Adi and others who had the ability and willingness to be trained and serve, traveled to preach as lay pastors. They planted hundreds of home churches and baptized and married many people outside the officially recognized church buildings. He accomplished positive results anytime, anywhere the opportunity arose.

Being among them, to be steeped in the culture, was why I had come. This was my first step to understanding whether there would be anybody to go with me to PC#3 so I could wander freely in and out of it without a Romanian chaperone.

Romanian believers are no different than any other Christ-followers. Some accept Jesus as their Savior simply to inherit eternal life. We claim He lives in us, but we share none of His burdens for the vast needs of those who are suffering all around us. Oh, we do some good works, but what we choose to give of ourselves and our resources only costs us what we can easily afford. While there are a few whose hearts are broken, and they move out into His pain for the hurts of the many, those people are few. Like churchgoers everywhere, we live respectable lives, but those who get out of the boat to walk on water are thought to be fools—mainly because we feel a little guilty watching them try. Few people accept the role of being a fool for Jesus. Adi was one of the few who didn't mind what others thought of him, and therein lies a part of the reason he allowed his heart to be open to our relationship.

Accepting Adi's invitation to return to Romania had been easy. I wrote earlier about wanting to meet the people and see Romania after the collapse of the Ceauşescu government as soon as possible, before they slipped the vestiges of Eastern European-style Communism. I wanted to experience the people and their culture before all of them became "Westernized." Time was short. By the time the next generation of Romanians grew to adolescence, the memories of places like PC#3 would be lost.

CHAPTER 10

Freedom to Roam in His Heart

Then I looked again at all the acts of oppression which were being done under the sun. And behold, I saw the tears of the oppressed and that they had no one to comfort them; and power was on the side of their oppressors, but they had no one to comfort them.

—Ecclesiastes 4:1

It was 1994, a year later, and I was back in Constanta, free to roam anywhere in Romania I chose to go and free to speak with any of her citizens who would return my interest in them. Such freedom of movement and access was a remarkable gift. Following as swiftly as it did on the failure of the Soviet Union and Romania to remain isolated from the rest of the world, it was surely predestined.

Two years earlier, the chance for Romania's citizens to have an open conversation with a Westerner would not have been possible without irresponsible risk. In fact, it would have been dangerous for me and the people I met to be seen by the Department of State Security, or, as it still referred to by Romanians who lived under its terror, Securitate.

The Departamentul Securitatii Statului was organized in 1948 with the help of the Soviet NKVD, the predecessor to the security organization known as the KGB. At its height, the Securitate had 25,000 or more employees, 11,000 agents, and 500,000 informers. In proportion to Romania's population of twenty-two million in 1956, it was one of the largest secret police forces on the Eastern bloc. Under Ceauşescu, the Securitate was one of the most brutal secret police forces in the world, responsible for the arrests, torture, and deaths of thousands of people.

In the years first following the revolution, if I uttered a greeting to Romanians in the US, their expressions would turn to a look of startled fear until I assured them my greeting was meant in friendship. Today when I speak to them, I get more a look of surprise. Romanian isn't a language commonly spoken outside its home country, and Romanians expatriates are a cloistered, tightly connected group who still mistrust a face that clearly isn't Romanian.

There is a colloquialism in Romania: "I have blue eyes." Adi used it once when I asked him how he knew so much about some matter that wasn't common knowledge. He said the Russians have blue eyes, Romanians seldom do, and Russians are KGB (or Russian intelligence agents). When I've used the expression in conversations in-country, it earns me a silent look that tells me they understand I have an insight into their culture and no further explanation is needed.

But if the darkness and sullenness of Romania and her people frightened me, walking their streets and wandering through their hospitals and orphanages so soon after their revolution left them visibly startled and suspicious. The effects of their oppression were still very present, even five years after Ceauşescu's overthrow. Those whose curiosity overcame their suspicion wanted to ask me questions, too, and I welcomed those moments. I was there to listen and learn, and my curiosity was voracious! It was an amazing window in time when the country had come to a dead stop, and in the ensuing quiet, those who would speak with me were as curious about my culture as I was theirs.

And it went both ways. During the first few years as I traveled back and forth from California to Romania, I would be met with a lot of questions. My Swiss acquaintances, finding out we'd been in Romania, would respond with "Oh, we're sorry." My American friends—with the images of the Romanian revolution still fresh in their minds—would ask me questions such as "Are things getting any better in Romania?"

The tone of people's questions referring to Romanians as a people could often be condescending—but not always. Sometimes it held curiosity, sometimes genuine sympathy and concern. I adopted a reflective listening posture with a neutral question of my own. "Better? In what way?"

This often prompted a response like "Yes, you know, now that Communism is gone, is their economy getting any better? Is the standard of living improving? Do the people want democracy? Do they embrace capitalism?" Later on, after PC#3 became Casa Viata Noua (CVN)—the House of New Life—the questions were couched in a different context: "Now that Communism is gone, is the government being helpful to you? Are the kids being adopted? Do their families take them back? How long do you intend to stay? What's going to happen to the kids? Will Romanians ever begin to share our beliefs, our values, now that they're free?"

I'd usually answer with: "When I went there the first time, the population was 23 million. Now it's 17 million. Those that can leave have left, and they don't look back. No, those who are still there and those who've left don't expect their lives to get any better." Then if their interest was more than just in passing, I would go on: "And Romanians are saying, 'Yes, we are trying to become more like you. But now that you have seen what life was like for us back then and what it's like for us now, why are you in such a rush to become more like us? Haven't you seen that socialism doesn't work?'"

Having had the benefit of seeing the metamorphosis of both the US and Romania between 1992 and 2022, it seems people everywhere want to find hope from the changes brought about by Romania's inclusion into the community of Western nations. Yet change from the outside never restores lasting hope.

And yet I still found myself hoping, along with my countrymen and the Romanians, that political and economic changes would restore hope to the lives of the orphans in PC#3 and those who cared for them.

When Jesus rode into Jerusalem to die for us, he knew His burden, and it's been said He wept because, reflecting on His children's futures, He said, "If you had known on this day, even you, the conditions for peace! But now they have been hidden from your eyes" (Luke 19:42). And I would go on to paraphrase His mission vis-à-vis verse 42 (perhaps to the horror of the theologians) by saying, "Because you don't know what it is that changes the heart and restores hope that will bring you new life. I'm going to have to show you." Self-sacrificial love can bring change that gives hope a chance of being found or restored. It was those people for whom I looked as I roamed Constanta, seeking people willing to sacrificially love the residents of PC#3. I couldn't singlehandedly bear the burden of the kids' lives of hopelessness. I still thought it should be a Romanian burden, and my role in supporting them would be vicarious.

So that being the case, perhaps the less oblique question I forced myself to ask was what was I going to do about PC#3? I thought that now that the obstacles to Romanians' freedom of choice had been removed, they would rush to heal their country's shame and redeem the lives of the orphans with reforms and internally funded relief measures. I believed the system that institutionalized unwanted children had been forced on them. How else to explain how something like PC#3 could be rationalized as a practical solution for too many children with no parents? If the pediatric holocaust taking place in hundreds of other institutions wasn't universally accepted as one of the many gross inefficiencies of their system, there might be some people willing to invest themselves in the aftercare of these unfortunates. Maybe, if I went back often enough, I might inspire a few of those people to take the initiative and do the work, starting with just one small place: PC#3.

The obstacle, however, was the vast despondency of Romania's people. Iain MacGregor paints a far more succinct picture of what I saw on my first few visits to Romania and what our guests from the Romanian church tried to share with us around our breakfast table over coffee. In his book *Checkpoint Charlie*, MacGregor writes of what three Western journalists witnessed of life on the Eastern side of the Berlin Wall before it came down. A life that in his words *"made the three of them recoil of the name [German Democratic Republic]."*

Because of their press credentials, Western journalists were among the few who could cross back and forth across the "death zone" separating West Berlin from the East with relative impunity. MacGregor wrote:

For the seventeen million East German citizens [and I could just as easily say the twenty-three million Romanians] *penned up in their country, with their everyday lives monitored, assessed, manipulated, and directed by as concealed and malevolent a force as the Stasi* [Romanian Securitate], *it was a form of daily humiliation. Unlike in the time of Stalin* [or the Romanian dictators, Gheorghiu-Dej and Ceauşescu], *people were not being rounded up, tortured and shot. The system perfected in the GDR* [and Romania] *was by the end of the 1970s far subtler and unobtrusive—to the point that the Stasi's political prison of Hohenschönhausen* [or Poarta Alba prison] *in Northeast Berlin was relatively unknown in the country. Unless you were unfortunate to be sent there …*

I was privileged to see the world my friends had lived in just before it changed. The cities were gray and colorless. They lay dark and unlit at night. There were no bright city lights or neon signs inviting the populace to come out to recreate after darkness fell or to identify with a brand like Coke or Pepsi. They had their lives, the ones the regime had given them, and they shouldn't hope for anything different without inviting punishment.

That was the life of the Romanians before December 1989. After the revolution, while I looked for people to share my burden for PC#3, I witnessed foreign investment slowly transforming Romania into a consumer-driven economy while my friends still continued to stoically endure a life of gross inefficiencies. They waited for improvements to health care, cheaper electricity, food, gasoline and diesel fuel, more reliable hot water, better telephone service, and choices of clothing, and they still dealt with the absence of restaurants and cars. Meanwhile, their meager State salaries could not pay for the

Western luxuries that did arrive. And yet despite the deprivation, humiliation, and their disappointment that the US didn't rush in with a new version of the Marshall Plan and its promised prosperity, most of them had learned to accept their bland lives with good humor and laugh it all off with the expression, "It takes a lot of time to live in Romania."

Too much time, to be truthful. Those I met were so occupied with adjusting to their new normal, I learned not to expect most of them to look back to find the children for whom political and economic change meant nothing. A few people saw them. Relief agencies saw them as an opportunity to bring reforms and educational programs that would result in donations if properly marketed. A few Romanians in the care system attached themselves to those relief budgets, acting as gatekeepers to increase their salaries. But no one offered self-sacrificial love to bring change and restore hope except for some pitifully few brave ones who gave their time as professionals or volunteers. Even these had no resources, no funding to provide overhead or to bring about permanent change to the deteriorating living conditions in the orphanages.

And even if they had had a sponsor with money to provide a sovereign stand-alone program to give a new life to the orphans, how would they separate my PC#3 orphanage from the hundreds of other orphanages under the Gulag's authority so we could operate it independently? It wasn't possible in such a tightly controlled, top-down culture, and my hope languished, since I had no idea things would—or could—change. But God never leaves us completely alone.

CHAPTER 11

Going Deeper

"Whom shall I send, and who will go for Us?"
Then I said, "Here am I. Send me!"

—Isaiah 6:8

In the spring of 1994, I began the first of many trips back to Constanta and PC#3. I usually went alone. Adi's family took me in and cared for me as I roamed across the city or spent my days with Adi. It's important to note here that the gift of their friendship and the ways in which they looked after me were why I was able to grow roots in Romania and later on build a mission. Apart from the wonderfully rich fellowship we shared, it's no exaggeration to say I was way out on a very thin limb, even if I wasn't alone. Trusting the Spirit's leading was the only way to be available to hear His directions and find peace in the face of the risks. The family had my back, so I was free to risk falling, knowing I had a safety net.

From 1993 to 1998, whenever I boarded the plane and left Zurich for Bucharest, I entered a communications blackout, leaving behind connections to home and the conveniences that we took for granted in the West. I wouldn't know if Cynthia had emergencies with the kids or if my own building projects had problems. In the event I was in an auto accident or had an accidental bite, scratch, or needlestick from being around the kids with HIV, I wouldn't have access to safe, quick medical care until I landed again in Switzerland. Antivirals, which don't cure HIV but slow the virus's onset if administered immediately, were not available in Constanta. It would've been three days to be extracted, fly to Zurich, and be treated. We think nothing of HIV now as a personal threat because it's understood and treatable. Only the COVID-19 virus shares the immediacy of people's fears the way HIV did then. Being isolated, though, was a good thing, because it kept me in the moment, free of distractions. In fact, it was a blessing, because I was forced to trust God with my uncertainties.

Adi and his family taught me how to get around in the city. I rode the trams or bought a cab for a dollar a day. At dinner each night, they tutored me in basic language skills and how to count and change money, and they offered rebuttals to the assumptions I'd made about the people I met that day.

When I explored the infectious disease hospital or PC#3, I always brought small boxes of chocolate, and I affected a sociable countenance with the people below the level of the directors or departmental heads. Visitors typically wanted to meet with the Romanians in directorship roles. I had already met the directors or department heads in both places in my initial tours, and I had kept up with them. But I wanted to find the ordinary, less "tour-worthy," and lesser-known people who would be open to teaching me things—or if I touched a nerve with my questions, shut their doors. In either case, I would learn something, and I would use it to cross-reference the truth about what really took place before agencies or foundations from the West became involved in their treatment programs or their support efforts.

I was fascinated by what was not being disclosed. After only two visits, I knew little of what was expected of me. I sensed there were expectations to come, but I needed time to know what was below the surface of the suffering that lay spread out in the open. Christ's apostles asked Him, "Why are we going up to Jerusalem?" and He told them, "It's not time for you to know yet." On a hot, humid night on one of my earliest visits, I lay awake in the summer heat sweating onto my sheets, unable to sleep, asking Him, "Why do You have me here, and why am I so happy?"

For the relationships.

"What does that mean?" I asked, and nothing came back.

I discovered where the care centers and hospital wards were that weren't open to visitors; only the patients and their relatives were permitted entry. I came and went, and it was like I was invisible.

Adi and I both spent time at PC#3, and after our visits we'd usually drive away not saying very much about what we'd seen. When we did speak of it, like most men, we'd hypothetically problem-solve the most glaring deficiencies, such as the decrepit condition of the building itself. But our talk only came to speculating about a wish list of building repairs we'd make if we were in charge. We were dreaming. What could we do? How could two guys take back a government hospital annex and rebuild it, support it, and staff it so that it became livable?

The more visits I made to PC#3, the easier it was for me to disappear into the building unnoticed. Apart from the infectious disease hospital, no other place held as much of my attention. I wanted to know each child's name. I would sit quietly in a hallway and watch. I studied the interplay between the kids and the staff to learn the staff's habits of caring for the kids. I spent hours with the director while she confided her heartbreak over the lack of adequate clothing, laundry, food, and staffing, unable to cook, clean, and care for fifty children. About a third of the kids had profound special needs that broke my heart. They should have been in a facility dedicated to caring only for them. Often the director would lose her stoicism and cry in frustration. She felt responsible for everyone who worked or lived there, for what she felt was her inability to move the hospital administration's indifference to their suffering. There were reasons the poor conditions were allowed to continue ... but what were those reasons?

My relationships with the kids and the staff in the hospital wards at PC#3 and some others in a few of the managed care settings grew. I began to learn their names and was able to keep up with their circumstances. We—the nurses, doctors, kids, support staff, and I—began to recognize each other, but our ability to communicate was still limited.

The kids shared one thing in common: they were the survivors. Born in Romanian hospitals, they had survived childbirth and then the pediatric wards where they were wrapped in sheets and left alone. Most of them had survived the neglect of being left in their cribs until they were old enough to walk. Most never knew their parents. Many had no birth certificates. No one could remember where or when they were born. They hadn't died yet from the complications arising from their HIV status.

Their ages ranged from three to ten years. Naturally, each possessed unique qualities, and each child longed to be known. But they hadn't learned how to express their needs appropriately.

For those who couldn't speak, their inability to express themselves frustrated them and us too. It would be safe to say that most if not all of them suffered from Reactive Attachment Disorder (RAD) and Attention Deficit Hyperactivity Disorder (ADHD). To diagnose and appropriately treat thirty or so kids, some with special needs, would have required several very skilled clinicians working several days a week with the kids, talent we didn't have access to. But these kids were the survivors. They were the tough ones. They had clung to life in isolation, competing for the attention of their ward attendants in a room full of other kids all seeking the same thing. Any progress in bringing these kids out of their confusion would take years of care. That was plain.

We often use the phrase "unspeakable horrors" to refer to others: the ones who initiated the rape of Nanjing, the Holocaust, or the Killing Fields of Cambodia. It's *those people* who are capable of such acts, not us. I now use "unspeakable" to describe the murky or pained silence with which I was met as I gently pushed against the Romanians' silence in response to my questions.

It took time for me to encourage people to share their histories and recollections with me. Some never would speak. Those who did expressed their feelings slowly in small anecdotal reflections. During numerous conversations, Adi and his family remained guarded, except Adi who would say, "There isn't a family in Romania that hasn't been touched by the orphanage system." Or "You have no idea what you're asking people to do." Others, often in grief, were open to sharing their regrets, their hearts hungering to find peace. But in that culture, there were no avenues to finding peace. Not for many years was anyone comfortable enough with me to explain how the method of "culling" the population of unwanted children worked.

I said I wanted to know each of the children in PC#3 in order to touch the source of their anger and calm it. The hurts were vast. Have you ever been so hungry you screamed for relief, and when no one came, you stole someone else's food? And when that person screamed at you and grabbed at you to take back their food, you beat them to death to stop the noise and keep the caregivers from coming around and giving the food back to the person you took it from? Have you been left in the care of someone who, when they saw what you had done to the smaller person, beat you in return, only not to death because they could lose their job if their deeds were discovered?

Have you ever craved attention or a hug so badly you screamed for the attention of anybody who would come and, when they came, clung to their leg and wouldn't let go until they slapped you off, picked you up, and flung you through the air into your crib?

In these early years, I received only oblique glimpses of the terrors the kids experienced, and since they couldn't tell me what had happened to them, and I was still just a visitor, I'd leave for home with the same frustration and anger I'd felt in Zurich after my first visit.

A few of the kids possessed an unusual dignity. They had a measure of maturity that allowed them to forgive us. These kids thought of everyone else first. Rather than snatching a gift or some food and running away with it, they offered it to the others, then they smiled and thanked us for bringing it. This was very unusual behavior.

Andrea and Nicoletta were two such unusual young ladies. They lived in Laura's House under the care of Osana Foundation, a not-for-profit foundation that Adi began with a Finnish foundation. They were probably twelve years old. Their "mother" was my friend Daniela. Daniela managed the care of ten or so kids in Laura's House. They called her "Dana Banana" because she brought them bananas. It was Dani who called me during a visit in February 1999 and asked if I'd like to visit Nicoletta in the hospital. She had progressed from HIV to AIDS and was dying.

As we drove to the infectious disease hospital, Dani told me Andrea had been spending days and nights in the infectious disease hospital ward caring for her friend. When we arrived, Andrea was feeding Nico ice chips. Both girls were conversant and wanted to talk a little about how they were managing. Dani translated for me. The nurses left us alone. Nico was in the advanced stages of the illness and couldn't bend her arms to feed herself. Her lips and mouth were covered in sores, eating was unappetizing, and drinking was painful. Trying to hold a glass was too hard for her to manage alone, so Andrea fed her ice chips and spoon-fed her what little soup Nico could manage to get down. Sleep was difficult too. She smiled while telling us these things. She never complained, and Andrea didn't either; they wanted to know how we were.

Nico had drawn a picture for me using colored pencils. A sun beamed down on two butterflies, one red and one yellow, fluttering above green grass and flowers of blue, red, and orange. On it she wrote, "Nicoletta pentru, Hud" (From Nicoletta, for Hud). She died February 8, 1999. Given her pain, I don't know how she managed to draw that picture. Maybe Andrea drew it for her. Sometime in the future I'll ask.

The infectious disease hospital was a dark and forbidding-looking building, standing off by itself on a street corner near the railroad station. It always looked like a big black heart, and each time I looked at it, I felt dread. No one will acknowledge the number, but it's likely that hundreds of dying children had lived there. I had a maudlin fascination with the images of the suffering I saw when I searched about in its hallways, hoping to be salt and light to patients and staff that I met. But the cynicism of the doctors and nurses who worked there was contagious. It was an evil and terrible place.

By acting innocently, I was able to move about the hospital freely. The guard's box at the street entry was just inside the main gate. It actually had one of those wooden horizontal posts painted with red and white stripes like you see in the war movies, and it was staffed by soldiers with AK-47 rifles. Visitors and contractors offered small favors to the soldiers in exchange for access to patients. I became a familiar figure to the guards, who'd seen me from earlier visits with the doctors and nurses, and they would give me a casual glance, sometimes a nod and a smile as I ran by them and up the stairway to the fourth floor where the pediatric wards were. They might've thought I had some kind of "get past go" pass issued by the doctors and the head nurse.

One day I met Sefa ("Sheffa"), the head nurse in the pediatric ward. She had a huge voice and the reputation for being a tyrant. Medical staff said she was tough, even cruel, and I was told she ran the ward with brutal efficiency.

Nurses and their assistants felt intimidated by her. Like the others, I found Sefa to be brusque and loud. Yet each time we met, she would share with me her experiences working in the hospital. I sensed an opening, and I made a point of bringing her small boxes of chocolates on my hospital visits.

In the Romanian health care system, efficiency trumped compassion—and Sefa was efficient. If we sat too long in her office it would look suspicious to the skeptical staff, so it became our practice to walk through the ward together while she talked and I asked questions. She spoke some English, and we were able to understand each other. While we walked, she recalled the suffering and deaths of so many children. It was obvious to me that she had suffered from her experience of being trapped in a workplace setting that did not allow compassion.

As usual, at dinner with Adi and his family, I told them my stories about the hospital. One night they politely told me Sefa's real name wasn't Sefa; it was something else. *Sefa* is the feminine form of *chief* in Romanian.

I was surprised one day when instead of greeting me with the customary kisses on both cheeks, Sefa took my arm and turned me toward her office, pointing me to a chair to sit. She spoke with an uncharacteristic softness.

"What am I supposed to tell them?" It was more like a plea than a question.

"Who is 'they'?" I asked.

"Open the door and look out there carefully so they don't see you. Do you see that couple out there sitting on the bench with the child between them?"

In the lobby there was a young couple with their little girl. They sat patiently on a bench, their backs leaning up against the wall. Their countenance was stoic. They had come for Sefa's diagnosis of their daughter's condition.

I nodded and asked again, "Who are they?"

She said to me: "I can't do this anymore. I know these people. The mother's a pediatrician, she's been a colleague of mine here in the ward. Her child was given a tainted vaccine, and now she's HIV-positive. I can't bear to tell them. How many more times do I have to do this?" Sefa took my hands in hers and sobbed.

Like her, I had no answers.

I continued to meet with Sefa on subsequent hospital visits. She allowed me to go anywhere in the hospital I wished. I visited the wards, waiting rooms, and treatment areas. She eventually built a playground for the children in the wards who were well enough to go outdoors. She was so proud of it. And then she was gone. I had no idea where or why. I asked Adi if I might visit her in her home, but it never came about. There was a history between them that wasn't explained. My perspective allowed me to see her in a different light. It was easy for me, an outsider, to be the listening ear she needed to express her regrets and sadness without fear of judgment.

I continued to visit the hospital. On one visit to the pediatric ward, I wandered in to find a boy lying on a gurney in the center of the room. He looked to be about eight or nine years old. He had brown hair and brown eyes. What captured my attention about this one was that he was restrained at the wrists and ankles by strips of cloth from a torn bedsheet. The gurney had no sides on it, so without the restraints he would have rolled off onto the floor and pulled out his IVs. The room was stifling hot, which may have explained why he was dressed only in a diaper.

The floor was a faded, gritty vinyl under my shoes, and it was rolled up along the edges of the walls in places. Here and there, tiles were missing from the walls. The sight of the little boy, the smell of unemptied bed pans, and the fouled beds of unattended children added to the sadness of the place. The windows were closed, and flies buzzed lazily in the stillness. Outside the room the nurses smoked and socialized at card tables in the hallway.

Bottles of solutions hung over the boy. He was being fed intravenously through oversized needles better suited for adults. His head was turned away from the door, and he lay awake, lost in his own world, completely alone. His abdomen was so grossly distended, he took on the shape of a pregnant woman.

A nurse who knew me caught my questioning glance and answered it with, "From hepatitis, and he cannot hear you. He is deaf and mute, from encephalitis." That explained the diaper. Like the other children in the ward, he was a prisoner to his gurney. The diaper was changed on a schedule—not necessarily when it needed to be.

A little boy with HIV, hepatitis, and post-encephalitic symptoms, he was suffering from the effects of all three.

I moved closer to the boy, but he was facing away from me, unaware of anyone else around him because he didn't want to be aware of us. "Ah, he's in the fog," I thought to myself. "Cool, safe, escaping from the pain of isolation and neglect. No way to reach this one."

"Where are his parents?" I asked the nurse.

"He is alone," she said. "His parents don't know where he is. He's HIV. The State cares for him now."

I bent down, my face close to the boy's, and blew my breath across his right cheek. He turned his head toward me, and our eyes met. I whispered, "I love you. That's all I can do for you now." I didn't stop to think if he could understand English; I wasn't thinking practically. For the moment, he wasn't alone in the gray shroud; there was someone there to see him. Who was it?

I love you. That's all I can do for you now. The words echoed in my head, and in that instant, my conscience shrank back from the promise I had just uttered. The clarity of the promise, and how it was made without any hesitation, startled me. A promise had just been made to a dying child that relief would come to him and to the children in PC#3, but these weren't my words, spoken with tenderness and love and with commitment and fortitude. Where did they come from?

In the fraction of an instant, my conscience remonstrated to my soul: *That's presumptuous of you!* But the voice in my soul answered, *You also heard Me say 'I love you.' That love is real and it's from Me; it's eternal. I'll welcome that little boy in a few days, and in the future, My love will manifest itself to the others through you. Leave now and be at peace.*

The Spirit had made two promises that day: one to the little boy and one to me. *Very soon I'll be there to welcome you into the kingdom, little boy, and in the future, Hud, I'll be there with you when you return to help the others. For now, that's all I can do for either of you.* Like the boy, I wasn't alone in the hospital. Abraham's people believed they carried their Yahweh with them in the Ark. Then in a new and more personal covenant, His Son promised we would carry His presence with us in our hearts. If we listen for Him, even greater things will we do in His name, by faith. That's startling stuff when we study it in our catechisms, but it's even more startling when He reveals Himself and we see Him working through us.

Now, when we drive by the infectious disease hospital, I glance at it, but that's as far as I allow myself to be distracted from the agenda at that moment. For me, some very holy moments took place there, and the memories of them pop up every now and then. But I don't reflect on them openly to the people I'm with—or more than that, write about them—because they're personal.

That's all I can do for you now.

CHAPTER 12

Making Tents with the Jesus People

*And he found a Jew named Aquila … having recently come from
Italy with his wife Priscilla … and because he was of
the same trade he stayed with them, and they worked together,
for they were tent-makers by trade.*

—Acts 18:2-3

It was while I was back for the third time in 1993 that I began to learn more about the life and practices of my friend Adi. I was hoping to further our relationship because I had an agenda that required his services. The job I had for him was directing the lives of the staff and residents of PC#3, and I would support him. Of course, Adi's agenda was different. He saw me as the driving force behind revamping PC#3, but neither of us could disclose our agenda to the other because they were goals that were too far out of reach. We had to wait.

"It's true. We arrange our relationships for purposes of mutual convenience," Adi would say several years later. "Friends are friends for a season and when that season or need is over, the friendship is over."

It was true, I did have a reason for befriending him. I'd had other convenient relationships for self-serving purposes, and when those services were no longer needed the relationship ended. Adi had too—we all do. But I also have lifelong relationships with friends that I treasure, and we go through many seasons together with those friends. So several years later, after PC#3 had become the House of New Life (Casa Viata Noua in Romanian or simply CVN), and Adi told me our friendship had had its season—thus he considered it over—I told him: "That may be true for you, but it isn't true for me. I'm cautioning you now—at some time in the future when you look back to see what it is that has its teeth firmly embedded in your backside, it will be me. I'm not going anywhere." I thought he was protecting himself (hence the candor).

It was also on this third trip when I met another one of the many seekers who came to Constanta looking for my friend. It amazed me how people found out about him. There were no websites then, and he wouldn't have published one anyway. What would it have said? *Adi: Seek first the kingdom, and I'll connect you to the people with the key to it.* All strictly from word of mouth, Adi was sought after by evangelical entrepreneurs and evangelists as well as real-life businesspeople purely looking for business opportunities. He had a reputation for being a man who could get things done and make connections, so despite having never left the country but once to see us, the network of people who knew of him was international.

"The Seeker" was one of those men who came looking for Adi's help. He came representing the business interests of the Jesus People USA. Headquartered in Chicago, these self-admitted onetime "hippies" with addictions had, for the most part, cut their hair, gotten clean, and coalesced around a mutually supportive Christian lifestyle based on the early church model described in Acts. We would never have guessed that the advocacy of one of their members would lead us to see how PC#3 could be transformed and become the House of New Life. It was while JPUSA was performing their due diligence on the proposed venture that the same person who in the beginning was the most vehement skeptic of the venture, and who was opposed to any such partnering of JPUSA with Adi in a building supply business, subsequently came to live in Constanta as the venture's strongest advocate.

Jesus People USA was a community that morphed from the former parentless, disenfranchised street kids who survived the '60s into a communal "family" on Chicago's north side. These were kids who might have been found in Haight-Ashbury or other city neighborhoods during the Age of Aquarius—wherever street people found a shared need. They were, in effect, kids disenfranchised from their families who'd found Jesus. Most had recovered from substance abuse of some kind and in their mutual afflictions, intuitively formed their own great big extended family to replace what they'd lost or never had.

JPUSA could easily be described as one of the best attempts I'd seen to replicate the Acts church of the New Testament. They were believers in Jesus. Their community was an earnest attempt at an egalitarian-evangelical-socialist society. To support themselves, they began a general contracting business, building cabinets and creating electrical wholesale building supply businesses. With funds that exceeded their living expenses, they sheltered and fed the homeless and operated drug and alcohol recovery programs. I visited some of their projects and was impressed. Whenever possible, some of those who experienced successful recoveries in their programs found jobs in JPUSA's businesses.

The Seeker had come to Romania in 1993 to find a less expensive source of gypsum board. Instead, he found an investment opportunity in Adi's vision of a wholesale building supply and contracting business. Adi wanted a business that was ready to supply materials for the explosion of building projects in post-revolutionary Romania. What Adi needed was seed money—operating funds until his venture's revenue allowed him to pay back his loans. What the Seeker and JPUSA needed were greater profits to support their community, but they didn't have the seed money to start more businesses either. So in February 1994, the Seeker asked Adi to visit Chicago because JPUSA had found an investor.

Adi phoned me to tell me all this. He asked if I would come to Chicago to help him vet those in JPUSA who were vetting him, and so I went. We were met in Chicago by a former member of the Constanta Baptist Church. This man had moved his family from Constanta. Adi had been his youth group leader at the church. This fellow had a car, something most of the individual members of the Jesus People didn't have, to drive us to JPUSA's communal residence. The JPUSA community lived in a hotel they had purchased out of bankruptcy, and for two days and nights we hung out with them in their extended family building.

We visited their businesses, ate in the communal dining hall, toured their outreach and recovery projects, and met their leadership. Bob and his wife were our informal hosts. They lived in a suite of rooms allocated to them on account of their three kids. Others had more or less space depending on their needs. Bob's position with the community was that of a business leader; he performed due diligence for potential business ventures for the community. Bob is very bright. He's a gentle person, soft-spoken and thoughtful. I stayed up with him most of the first night talking about his marriage. I explained to him what it was like for me to live my life as a Christian "on the outside" of a place like their community—in a house, in a traditional home, with a family.

With several hundred people living together in one building as a large extended family, naturally differences of opinion will arise about how privileges are apportioned. To decide such matters, a committee of leaders adjudicated a consensus, and the parties would live with what the committee decided was equitable.

While I was there, a smaller committee went to a spaghetti dinner given by an entrepreneur at his house in an inner-city Chicago neighborhood. Adi and I attended with Bob, the Seeker, and one other man. The entrepreneur was to be JPUSA's investor for this project. He wanted to measure Adi's intentions for the business and explain his own conditions for seeding the Romanian opportunity.

I favored the opportunity because Adi needed the seed money. Bob did not and said so vehemently. In the car on the way to dinner, Adi and I listened to the conversation between the JPUSA principals. Bob saw the venture as a pipe dream. He hadn't been to Romania and didn't know Adi. Bob rightly felt that JPUSA had no business experience in Romania. JPUSA would need an auditor, but only someone from JPUSA with an objective view of the venture who could travel periodically to Constanta to conduct the audit. Once the business began, that person would likely be the Seeker because he had travel privileges, something only a few of the community enjoyed. Bob thought it unlikely that, after the venture was started, the Seeker would be quick to disassemble or course-correct something he'd originated if the business were failing or was in danger of corruption. From an earlier conversation with Bob, I knew that only a few in the JPUSA community were given the privileges of European travel and better familial living circumstances. So from the beginning, opinions about the Romanian venture were prejudiced.

That night at dinner, the entrepreneur gave Adi and JPUSA $200,000 to start their business in Constanta, with the proviso that net profits would fund projects to serve the needs of the poor in Constanta. He didn't want the money back.

Because Bob was so opposed to the idea of JPUSA in a Romanian business venture, in the fall of 1994 he was encouraged to travel to Constanta to see the possibilities for himself. While he was there, Adi took him to an orphanage. Bob's soul was reawakened. He came back to Chicago convinced that JPUSA needed to have a presence in Constanta, and that a member of the JPUSA community needed to be in residence to help Adi get the business started. That member would need to remain there for at least two years and audit it to avoid abuses and keep the vision on track. And so it was that Bob, his wife, and their three children moved into their own apartment in Constanta to find work with Adi. In May 1995, NARCOM (Nehemiah American Romanian Company) made its first sale.

Bob had had the same encounter as me in PC#3. He found Jesus among the least of the least looking back at him and beckoning for his company in Marolen's Casa Speranta, the House of Hope, in Constanta, Romania.

CHAPTER 13

Marolen Shares Her Light

For you were once darkness, but now you are light in the Lord;
walk as children of light.

—Ephesians 5:8

By October 1996, Bob and his wife had left their former JPUSA community and settled into their new life of independence as a sovereign family. But their new life also included other people, most of them members of a growing community of US expatriates and others who had come carrying a unique burden for Romania. It was as if someone had poked a hole in a bubble and created a vacuum that sucked people in from all over the world, even if the greatest number came from the United States.

Each of them had seen something in Romania they needed to touch. Romania's stark needs, exposed for the world to see after the revolution, drew evangelicals and others with charitable souls like a magnet. The people I met and their causes were as varied as the regions from which they had come: Texas, Delaware, the Carolinas, Arizona, Illinois, and California, just to name few.

Each of them without exception felt a call to be there. I had a cause, too, but I was still on the sidelines watching them. I still couldn't get my head around managing a problem as big as PC#3.

Bob and his family's Romanian experience was their first taste of adult life outside the limits of the JPUSA community, and now lights of awareness were coming on that were different for each of them. His wife loved exploring Constanta's culture. Bob's light was naturally for the children in the orphanages. In the year or so since coming to Constanta, each time I returned for a visit, Bob had been quietly asking me to go with him to see a place called Casa Speranta, but each time I refused him, keeping my focus on PC#3. Bob had seen PC#3, but his aversion to confrontation led him to a conviction that PC#3's kids were lost and irrecoverable. The infectious disease hospital had too strong a grip on their care. But on this visit, gentle Bob was adamant. "You have to come with me to see Casa Speranta and meet Marolen!"

Casa Speranta was the work of an American expatriate. Marolen had come to Constanta in the early '90s under contract to an American relief agency and had fallen in love with a group of kids. When her contract expired, Marolen decided to stay in Constanta to manage their lives. She couldn't abide what she foresaw for their future when her sponsoring foundation withdrew its financial support.

Marolen had guts! These kids were also HIV-positive. HIV then was misunderstood, and it was dangerous to be around the kids when they lost control of their tempers. Had she experienced a needlestick or been bitten or scratched by a child, she would've had to leave the country for an AZT injection, which would've been too late in coming. To stay in the Constanta hospitals then was, and still is now, a risky practice.

Marolen was a blonde force of nature with glasses, a loud east

Texas accent, and a propensity for chain-smoking Romanian cigarettes. As would become her habit, when Marolen saw Bob and me coming down the walk that led to her building, she met us at the front door with her Romanian assistant and led us back to an office piled high with papers and documents.

She explained to me how she had volunteered to work in Romania for a US NGO (nongovernmental organization) after watching a *20/20* segment on television. She walked us through the building like any mom showing off her house. Her vision was to deinstitutionalize the lives of her kids. She wanted each of them to emerge as individuals, so she ensured the kids had their own identity: toys, clothes, and beds.

To manage the anger that the kids would express after the abuse was lifted, she had divided the kids into "families," small groups of four to five kids, each group with two caregivers called "mamas." The mamas were with the kids in their respective families 24/7. They did everything together as families. They went on trips out as families. A cook prepared the food, and the mamas went to the kitchen and brought it to their families. They ate their meals together in their own room as families do, not as the inmates of an institution.

Marolen had started a Montessori school, which she hoped would teach self-reliance and mutual respect for mamas and children alike. And if uncontrollable anger ever broke out, or a mom was stressed to the point of losing her temper, they went to the other mamas in the house for help rather than succumbing to the Reactive Attachment Disorder (RAD) tactics of the kids. Hitting a child would get a staff member dismissed immediately. The kind of unhealthy stimulation that had damaged the children had to be unlearned if their individuation was to begin again with any hope of success. Nameless, forgotten human detritus would find dignity and love before they died.

Marolen's ingenuity was amazing. She started Casa Speranta with nothing. To provide for the kids above the bare subsistence level, she had to find resources and commodities from empty Romanian shelves. If she needed more food, medicines, and clothing to keep up with the needs of an emerging "family," her only resources were her hope and ambition. She coached the mamas, comforted and treated the kids with extra medical care, and cajoled the Romanian health care system to get her more of everything.

As we toured her home, I caught myself staring at objects that seemed out of context with a board-and-care home for sick and abandoned children. I saw testimonials and letters of thanks from the Marines, Navy, and other branches of the American military service. There were squadron patches and the names of US Navy ships, along with photos of American servicemen. The strong military presence was such an incongruous connection to a shelter for children on a backstreet in an out-of-the-way place.

"Marolen, who are all these military people?"

"Oh, they help me. They're my partners! They help me take care of these kids."

"How did they find you?" I asked her.

"Oh, I found them!" She told me the soldiers and sailors were personnel from the US Mediterranean fleet. They would never have found her place on shore leave, so out of desperation, she went looking for them.

Marolen had gone down to the port of Constanta when ships of the US fleet would come in. She stood on the docks waving an American flag and yelled at the sailors on board their ships. "Hey, you guys, I'm an American. I've got a place here with a bunch of Romanian orphans. They're sick and hungry, and I need your help!" Eventually, after she convinced a few shore parties to come see what she was yelling about, the trickle became a routine mission of support.

Like most Americans, they came back repeatedly and volunteered to help around the house. The sailors and Marines brought things the house needed and made donations of food and cash. Extensive relationships developed, which eventually worked themselves up the American chain of command to the US naval attaché to Romania. I don't know for sure how she met him, but it was his job to know about and report back to his superiors what was going on with American activities in Romania. He learned of Marolen's work at Casa Speranta from fleet officers, and he became a powerful advocate not just for Marolen but for the orphans themselves. He followed the activities at PC#3 and other NGOs too.

On this first visit, I watched and listened to Marolen. I was taking her emotional temperature. She'd been a mother and protector of her fragile charges for four years, living on the edge of a bare-bones existence. If she ran out of food, clothing, or medicines, she had to go find them. Her circle of friends there was small, mostly her staff of Romanian mamas interspersed with occasional visits from US military personnel. Internet access didn't exist then, and being a "tough cookie," she downplayed her own needs. She had seen a lot of her kids die, most of them unnecessarily. She was fragile emotionally and exhausted physically. On this particular visit, when her energy finally ran down, she stopped talking and became quiet. I asked her, "So Marolen, who listens to you?" Standing there next to me, she began to cry and for several minutes I held her while she sobbed.

Like most of us, Bob had found himself becoming invested while sitting among the kids of Casa Speranta. He loved Marolen and her staff for their empathy and advocacy. But he loved the children. Casa Speranta could get along, but they were struggling. Bob wanted to do more for them. Fifty dollars a month would have made a difference. He brought me there because he wanted my financial support for Casa Speranta. From his JPUSA community outreach perspective, I could understand why. Support for Casa Speranta would be an in-place outreach; nothing new needed to be created. That appealed to him, and Marolen needed it.

Marolen was such a strong personality that collaboration wasn't likely. By partnering with her, nothing new in the orphanage support system would have been added, and I did not want to be directed away from the needs of the kids in PC#3. I am a principal. I never wanted to just write checks. I wanted to originate the work and then do it.

That her kids were HIV-positive was not her focus. I felt the same. Marolen and I knew that almost all the kids in PC#3 and Casa Speranta happened to have HIV, but that wasn't our only concern. Being an HIV activist implies being attached to a cause. I had a cause, an agenda, but I didn't want to simply support a cause. I wanted to gather the kids around me and love them as if they were my own. She felt the same. Before I saw her Casa Speranta model of separating the kids into small "families" and budgeting and staffing around that model, I had not been able to envision how to manage the rage the kids would express once the lids of abuse and neglect were lifted.

There is an egocentric, entrepreneurial quality about the people who begin projects in relief work. They are leaders. Anyone who can see a need, has a vision for a different outcome, and has the temerity to personally follow through rarely collaborates. I hadn't yet found that vision or seen a mission yet for PC#3. I wanted my kids' lives changed, but I did not know how to do it. That day with Marolen and Bob at Casa Speranta, the light came on. I saw it, and I walked into it.

CHAPTER 14

We're Going to Have to Take That Place Over

The kingdom of heaven is like a treasure hidden in the field,
which a man found ... and from joy over it he goes and sells
everything that he has, and buys that field.

—Matthew 13:44

The front door to PC#3 would usually be found standing open, but one day in October 1996, it was locked. The weather begins to turn cold in October, so the closed door made sense, but not the lock. Access to the building was being denied.

Yet a blunt message at this level of management didn't come as a surprise. The nurses and their helpers had been giving away my presence by making comments under their breath whenever I was around lately, as if they were asking each other, "Should he still be in here?" On an earlier visit, the previous director had introduced me to her impending replacement and said that I could expect dwindling access to PC#3. The new one was almost my height, confident, and when I tried to be cordial toward her, she gave no signs of having any interest in having help or wanting to collaborate. The new director carried the demeanor of a warden—

an odd role for a caretaker of children—whereas her predecessor had been more like the head mother in a children's home.

We knocked at the door to get the attention of the staff. Our presence drew the attention of the new director, who responded by shouting at us from behind the door. "Don't come back here again! If you do, we'll call the police! Go away now. You are not welcome! If you don't leave now, we will call the police!"

A warden indeed. I wasn't surprised. I had gone back expecting to find either access or no access, and now I knew which one it was. The moment I'd expected had come, and the choice of what to do next was mine.

Now, imagine this scenario, as expressed by the imaginary mother of one of the children living in PC#3.

You're a parent and by coincidence you are standing at the front door of PC#3 alongside two strangers: me and Adi. You're not the least bit interested in our reasons for being there. You're there because a few weeks ago a stranger had called, and when you heard the reason for her call, the shock of the words she spoke to you caused your knees to buckle. The caller told you that your child, whom you haven't seen in five years, is living in the building where you're now standing, on the other side of that heavy door steel door that stands locked in front of you.

Maybe the two men next to you know something you don't. Maybe they can help you get into the building to see your child. You ask: "What is this place? Why won't they let me in? They said my baby's in there. They took her from us five years ago. We didn't know anything was wrong, but when I brought her to the doctor, she told me, 'We need to keep your child for further observation.' I had no choice. If I didn't agree to let them keep her, she said she would take her anyway. I came back to take her home, and that's when the doctor told me my baby had died. But the person who called me last week told me it's not true, that she's alive. Are they all lying to me, the doctor and now these people? I have to get in there to get my child! Can you help me, please?"

Your child, along with hundreds of others, had been infected with HIV from a tainted vaccine shortly after birth, administered by a pediatrician who is herself threatened with a demotion or reassignment if she questions the department heads. To avoid being culpable, those same people took your child, and five years later, you think she may be alive. You've heard rumors about what happens to children in these places, but you looked away—it wasn't your problem, your child was dead.

Now it's possible your child has been kept in the conditions like the ones I described. Your child, along with the other kids, has scabies, is hungry and undernourished, while the virus is accelerating her death from weight loss. Clothing is interchangeable and non-gender specific; it just needs to fit because it's not important if the child is a boy or a girl. Your child may have been exposed to pedophiles for a fee paid to the staff who failed to mention to the abuser that the child has HIV. Your child has special needs from being neglected in the nursery. No matter what, your child will die, but unless you intervene, she will die alone.

Your child is innocent and so are you, but they won't let you go into the building to comfort her. You want to ask the people in charge of her care, "What kind of people are you that you do these things to my child?" But they won't let you in, and if you persist, they threaten to call the police to take you away and quiet you.

Maybe you were expecting a happy story—or worse, maybe I was. I'd offered myself to work in-country, but my sponsors from the first trip weren't interested. They wanted me to give cocktail parties to generate donations. They'd pulled their support out of

PC#3; they wanted their donors for another need. I offered to help the staff at PC#3, and they weren't interested. When I went back to Constanta to see if anybody there wanted to step up and help, I wasn't expecting to meet antipathy, or worse, open hostility for offering to help sick and dying children. I was at least expecting mild gratitude, but that was because I didn't know enough about the culture yet, and my thinking was skewed by my expectations.

Adi and I walked back to his car to collect our thoughts. After being threatened at the door and kept from the children, I sat there seething.

As I sat there in Adi's car, the same furious indignation I'd suppressed in Switzerland returned to me. There is often imposed on us the image of a gentle Jesus who always keeps the peace. Peace? Really? After seeing this? These were my children. I didn't just see the image of Jesus flipping over the tables of the money changers in the temple in Jerusalem. I felt His anger at the profligate priests in the temple, gatekeepers coming between God and His children, profiting from their corruption and the pollution of a holy place. It infuriated me that the hospital staff would desecrate the place where Christ suffered alongside the children and allow people to pervert the lives of these innocents. The emotions I felt that day ignited a terrible resolve to throw open PC#3's front door and gather the children around me to say to each one of them: "Come here. You're safe now. They are never going to do that to you again."

And yet, where would the people come from to help me to live out my indignation and redeem the lives of the kids in PC#3? I was back in the same corner. Could I go home and leave responsibility to the locals? If a person challenges the justice of a situation, they tie that person up in red tape. I once heard a government tax auditor say to my friend Adi, "I'm sorry, Adi, but the government must eat too. Don't try to deny us our food."

Yet, even facing these obstacles and frustrations, in October 1996 came several turning points. I had finally been locked out of the building. From then on if I wanted to gain access to the children, it would have to be as a principal, not as a visitor. I had seen Marolen's Casa Speranta. I would replicate her model and transform PC#3's chaos into a home. With these thoughts in mind, I went home to California, confident of one thing: We would be led. God would come along and show us how to provide. He'd taken me this far; He would continue and give us what we needed to do what He had called us to do. And he did, beginning with the telephone call I made to Adi.

"You know something, Adi. If we're ever going to have a significant impact on the lives of those kids, we're going to have to take that place over."

"I know."

"Do you realize what we've just said?"

"Yes. I'm afraid so."

"OK. See if you can set up some meetings with the right people at the hospital, and I'll come over, and we'll see if we can get an agreement to take that place over."

When we marry, we step off into the unknown. We don't know how we're going to do life together; we have no idea how our lives will evolve, nor do we know how much time we'll have together.

Partners in mission commit to the same ambiguity. Adi knew Romania better than I did, but if Marolen's model at Casa Speranta was to be replicated, then needed the eyes of someone who didn't see PC#3's transformation though a Romanian lens. The idealistic foreigner had proposed to the local realist, and a third strand bound us for the work that was to come.

I wanted more than anything in the world to be responsible for the contents of a repulsive building because there was a treasure hidden inside it that no one else seemed able to see. When we were turned away at the front door, I was prepared to move heaven and earth to reclaim what belonged to me. That's what we're called to do: learn to do good, seek justice, reprove the ruthless, defend the orphan, plead for the widow. Those aren't just platitudes and not merely Isaiah's poetry. They were my marching orders. What follows are the matters that affected the direction Adi and I took to acquire the field—and once we had possession of it, how its forgotten treasure came to be known by people all over the world.

CHAPTER 15

Let Them Go

If you do this thing and God so commands you,
then you will be able to endure, and all these people also
will go to their places in peace.

—Exodus 18:23

In May 1997, I was back in Constanta to negotiate with the
hospital for the authority to care for the kids in PC#3. I had
begged God to open the eyes of some Romanian authority figure
to see the suffering of the kids and want to end it—or at the very
least, to see an opportunity to profit from it by negotiating a
transfer of authority and giving me the chance to end it.
Ironically, the first day of our negotiations, I missed the meeting.
I was so sick with anticipation and fear of being disappointed
that the stress overwhelmed me. I lay in bed all day with flu-like
symptoms that disappeared instantly when Bob and Adi told me
that the hospital negotiators had agreed to give our proposal
serious consideration.

"Maybe they didn't understand what I'm after," I told the guys.

"Are you sure they understood you?" During the meetings Bob hadn't said much, but in keeping with his character, personality, and language skills, Adi had led the discussion. Adi and I understood each other because he was able to think in English. When he interpreted for me, he would encourage me to not try and be too precise. We would laugh at each other as we began.

"Don't worry," he'd tell me. "Say whatever you need to say. I'll tell them what they need to hear."

By the Spirit and our intuition, we were able to hear each other's thoughts, allowing for the context and the timing of our circumstances—even when we weren't together. Then we'd double back in person or on the phone, and we'd ask each other, "Is that what you understood? Is that what you saw?" and we'd move on in lockstep.

Adi and I both wanted control of PC#3, but even so, I hadn't expected such an apparent willingness to talk from the other side. The proposal I made and intended to hold out for was a clear departure from what other foreign agencies who wanted access to the kids had offered in the past. What I wasn't offering to do was renovate the PC#3 building and then give it back to them after some years. And I wouldn't agree to modify the hospital's protocol for managing the kids' living conditions while working alongside hospital employees.

My offer was different for two reasons. One, I asked them to relinquish their responsibility for caring for the kids in PC#3 completely; and two, I would manage their care and pay for it until the need was no longer necessary, without any interference from the hospital administration or the doctor. Just to be clear, I wanted total authority to manage and pay for the long-term care of the kids. In our proposal we defined the duration of our service as perpetual or until there was no more need.

I've already said that PC#3 was a wreck of a building, virtually uninhabitable, and that the kids who lived in it needed better care. I intended to renovate their building to make it comfortable, habitable, and functional for the staff. I would start with the basics and move up the hierarchy of needs once the building was usable, including their food, clothing, hygiene, education, and nurturing. I intended to weed out and dismiss the abusers and the indifferent members on the staff. The new staff of caregivers would need training and support. Nurturing them was critical, too, since they would bear the brunt of the kids' anger after the abuse and neglect that controlled them was lifted.

At the end of a long, hot, humid day later that summer, Adi and I were in his flat, sitting side by side on his couch. He listened while I vented. "This is taking too long, Adi. The doctor is playing games! Yesterday on the bus ride to Cernavoda, where the doctor showed us another of her group homes, she told me the language in the recent draft was fine, and our taking over the place was a good thing to do. Today she tells us an agreement isn't possible because the State can't lease one of their buildings to a foreign entity and allow them to operate it. Today she says she needs government approval and doesn't know who to see or where to go to initiate the approval process. She knew this before yesterday, Adi, and those kids are getting sicker and they're starting to die. Did you see Ribana [a six-year-old girl]? She's really sick. We can't wait that long!"

"Hud, you have to understand something. You've thrown a big rock in a small pond."

"Adi, it can't be helped. Somebody here has to have a conscience!"

"Hud, it takes a lot of time to live in Romania."

As I've mentioned before, living in Romania has an oppressive downside, a weight that can't be understood or, more to the point, felt until you spend some time there. Even today you'll hear Romanians use this self-deprecating euphemism to describe what it's like to live in their country—but I had not heard them use the expression during my first trips. I heard it for the first time when Adi used it to help ease our frustration with the time it was taking to resolve an agreement with the doctor. Everyday citizens found it easier to just give in, rather than confront the bureaucrats. I'd experienced the truth of the expression to a lesser degree from customs officials when I landed in Bucharest with gifts for the kids. They liked to get a gift, too, and they made it easier to quickly get out of the airport if they got one. But until Adi said it in the context of our negotiations, I hadn't fully appreciated what it was like to live in Romania. Now it was affecting me too because I was no longer a visitor.

I had thought that for the past several weeks the parties had been negotiating in good faith, but in truth I was being played as a witness to a Kabuki theater act. PC#3 wasn't just the hospital's alone to give away. The pediatric caseload was being managed by the department head of pediatric medicine in the infectious disease hospital, but the building itself belonged to the hospital. The doctor had her own budgets and the hospital's other department heads had theirs, which meant the kids, as assets, were being cross-collateralized by both parties to generate income. So untangling and isolating those income streams was complicated and would take more time unless I agreed to subsidize one or both of their budgets in return for sharing operating authority. That meant becoming a third party to an agreement with the doctor and the hospital as partners and paying them both off, and I wouldn't agree to either. Knowing beforehand that this was what they'd ask for was the reason for the simplicity of my proposal.

Having reached this impasse in the negotiations, my other idea to break the logjam was to try and find a way to bypass both of them, to lump the hospital and the doctor together and leap over them by going to a higher authority. I'd have to present the doctor and the hospital as one entity because going over their heads wouldn't make them disappear. The hospital and the doctor each had nonnegotiable sticking points, and Adi knew what they were, but he wouldn't address them with me. During our friendship I accepted him as a product of the culture, and he did the same with me. I seldom let him know that I knew what he knew. That was when I began to realize that our peculiar ethnocentrisms—both his and mine—were driving our individual agendas. Same goal, different means.

To see if the hospital and the doctor liked each other, I had informally sought access to the hospital's administration heads and gotten to know them in the years leading up to where we were now in the negotiations. Earlier I had asked, "Why do You have me here?" and the Lord's response was *For the relationships*. I had learned that the hospital wasn't being reimbursed by Bucharest for the beds they administered, but the doctor was being paid some money for her caseloads by the government, as well as accumulating grant monies from her research efforts. The doctor, because of her expertise in pediatric infectious diseases, drew most of the attention from foreign donation sources in Europe and the US. Donors were eager to study and gather data using controlled cohorts of HIV-positive pediatric cases. She was the leader among the other department heads in generating financial support due to the demand for data within her field of expertise.

I concluded that perhaps the only way I could break PC#3 loose from her control was to exploit a professional jealousy between her and the department heads of the hospital. It wouldn't have been my first method of choice, because for the long-term health of our work there, animus and jealousy between the parties wouldn't be a good way to start a relationship. But I didn't want a relationship with either one of them, and once we were in place, if we stayed long enough (as I intended to), they'd retire and take their animus with them. That strategy and its outcome proved to be true, but the animus was unavoidable. God's timing of the move, however, was perfect.

My patience in negotiations brought the politics of the situation to light. If her exploitation of the kids was well known, I could go over her head for permission to take PC#3 and avoid being her partner. To remain in control, she may also have been speaking for the department heads at the hospital, offering to share income from her grants—I never knew. I was viewed as being arrogant for challenging the status quo.

Adi had said it best: "Hud, you've thrown a big rock in a small pond."

I had never intended to embarrass the hospital administration, but I would not curtail my actions even if the by-product of exposing malfeasance and correcting it led to their embarrassment. The doctor and the hospital seemed incapable of seeing themselves as culpable. What I was offering them didn't strike them as an offer to help them to overcome a failure. They simply saw it as a loss of income from the number of pediatric beds they were paid to provide and the research data being generated by the kids. I have tried to explain how radical our proposal was, as if any right-thinking hospital official would of course see the wisdom in giving away a portion of their franchise to an outsider—and a foreigner at that. But being culpable parties never entered their minds.

After a couple of weeks and a few more meetings that led

nowhere, I was out of time to stay in-country, so I flew home with no agreement. The negotiations had dragged on into the late summer. The doctor was playing for time and hoping our frustration would lead to a partnership with her foundation. While she backtracked, agreeing to terms one day, disagreeing to terms the next, the kids were getting sicker. Their conditions were deteriorating as rapidly as the Romanian government's budget for their support was shrinking. But I didn't care anymore; there was no goodwill to lose. I flew back to see if I could get some help from a prominent US NGO in Bucharest.

The man I met with was the newest in-country director for the NGO. In my efforts to remain accountable to my host organization, I would drop into their Bucharest office on our way to Constanta and say hello to each new director. By remaining close to them, I learned things that helped me stay current with changes in Romanian policy. This director was the third I'd met and one I enjoyed being with the most—he was a good guy. He was casual in demeanor and very smart, so I could be less formal in meetings with him than with his predecessors because we both wanted to learn stuff from each other. He was easier to be around and a better networker than the others, so I might have guessed he knew about my ongoing negotiations with the hospital and the doctor before I got there.

I explained to him what I wanted to do with PC#3 but that negotiations had stalled. I wasn't asking for financial support from him. I said I had no intention of embarrassing anyone in the system, I simply wanted to become part of the fabric of the support community and keep a low profile. He laughed off that comment, reminding me Americans tend to stand out in Romania, particularly in settings like Constanta. "And knowing you, Hud, you will stand out."

I told him I knew that and I really didn't intend to cause trouble. I thought it wouldn't be difficult to do a better job than the current hospital administration and staff. I would provide funds for the budget in return for the opportunity to prove my case. He knew underfunded government budgets were the reason the conditions in the orphanages and pediatric hospital facilities were deteriorating. When we asked the agency heads why they didn't have a budget for a need, they'd say, "Oh, we have a budget. But there's no money in the budget to fund the needs." I told him I knew the hospital didn't want to give up the beds, and I knew they weren't being paid for them because there wasn't money in the budget, so it would be a net gain for everyone in the system if I assumed the cost of the care.

The fact I wasn't asking for funding piqued his interest. I wanted his help rolling a rock that was begging to be sent downhill. I asked him if he knew anyone in the central health care system in Bucharest who might help me roll the rock down the chain of command to Constanta with a message to let the beds go. He smiled and picked up his interoffice phone and called a man into his office. He introduced me to a member of their staff who had been number two or three in authority in the Romanian Ministry of Health, so his list of contacts packed some weight. He was currently on the NGO's staff as a medical adviser.

After a pleasant meet and greet, the director gave the staffer a casual explanation of what the problem was and said my plans for PC#3 were worthy of their endorsement. The man thought he could help.

Right then and there in the director's office, the man called someone. I've never known to whom he spoke, but he and the other person spoke briefly in Romanian. Then after a few sentences I do remember his exact words in English. He finished by saying: "Don't be silly. Let them have it. You're not being paid for the beds now, and the government doesn't have any money to reimburse you, so you're not losing anything. If they want to play with some children, they'll pay for it, and we'll all make some money."

CHAPTER 16

The Palace

But I say to you, love your enemies ... And if you greet only your brothers and sisters, what more are you doing than others?

—Matthew 5:44, 47

Irony is an expression of one's meaning by using language that normally signifies the opposite.

It's a vast generalization to make, but I think it's safe to say that most people who know something about the country will agree that the Palace of the People is the quintessential icon of Romania. Yet when the true nature of its size, cost, and weight were disclosed following the revolution, calling it "the Palace of the People" became the very definition of ironic.

Its size—which is what sets it apart—has made it impractical for anything useful. The palace is one of the largest buildings in the world at more than 365,000 square meters. It's dwarfed by Washington, D.C.'s Pentagon at 610,000 square meters, but the criteria for choosing the winner depends on whether the standard is being set by a Romanian nationalist or by someone ashamed of how the building reflects Romania's recent history. The palace is so out of proportion that it dwarfs every other structure around it. Its cavernous interiors are so vast and it has so many rooms (more than a thousand) that the government couldn't find a use for all of them, so they thought they'd demolish it. That would've been too expensive, so they made it a monument. Only in the last few years has the Romanian Parliament found ways to gather in a few of its rooms.

Two entire Romanian mountains were lost providing the stone to build it. It's so heavy it sinks six centimeters a year. Twenty thousand workers were assigned to complete it, yet it was never finished.

During its construction, the work to complete the palace consumed 30 percent of Romania's annual budget. For a time, it was a lightning rod for attracting the people's anger at their leaders. Ceaușescu reallocated funds from the nation's budget to pay for their palace, while the working people and the abandoned children in the orphanage system suffered malnutrition. It was this reallocation that forced the number of children in the institutions to be arbitrarily reduced. Perfectly normal children were "culled" from their care settings and sent to one of the many Camin Spitals. These terrible places were the last stop in the State's system of care facilities for "irrecoverable" children, where they died.

After the revolution, the palace was said to be the Romanian people's symbol of why they had finally rebelled and overthrown the dictator and his wife. It was a reflection of an ego out of touch with reality. It's located on the highest promontory in Bucharest, so that from the grand balcony of the palace, the dictator Ceaușescu could look out over the Romanian capital and claim the nation and its inhabitants as his subjects. The scale of the grand Palladian avenue leading up to its grand entryway and the balcony was by design three meters wider and some distance longer than the Champs-Elysees, the famed avenue in France.

Compare it to the Grand Canyon. After you've seen it, try describing it to someone. You cannot. You can't take either of them in fully—not standing at the rim of the canyon nor standing in the palace's parking lot—you must go into them. But unlike the Grand Canyon, access to the palace is restricted. Ordinary citizens and foreign visitors alike have to make an appointment to gain entry. Very few people have seen all of it because that would take days. The rooms and warehouses that lie beneath the surface encompass more square footage than the building above ground.

Ironically, at one time the palace was a shameful reminder to the people of their suffering, but now it's a symbol of national pride. I've been asked, "Look what we could build. Could you do that?"

"If it's a symbol of national pride," I tell them, "don't go looking too far into your past." There are dry bones in the basement of this grotesque edifice, and no one I know wants to go looking for them. These days not all Romanians want to remember it as a symbol of a time when they all had jobs and everything was clean and orderly. Not like today.

But there is another palace in Romania. This one's in Constanta, and it, too, is an icon. Tourists won't remember it because it's not safe for them to be there. This one has never been the domicile of a political leader or a king, and ironically, like the more well-known palace in Bucharest, it is uniquely unsightly. Very few locals have been to the palace in Constanta because, like the People's Palace, access is limited. If you mention this palace to the locals as a point of interest, they will look at you askance and question your judgment. Their thinking is, "There is no good reason for us to visit the palace, so why would you want to go there?"

I've been inside both palaces. My experience in the Constanta palace was not what I expected.

This second building has lent its ironic reputation to a residential district in Constanta. I first learned of it when I overheard two of my expatriate friends, Gary and Ken, talking between themselves about going together to make a call on one of its residents. I thought it was a palace, but their intonation when they spoke the word "palace" gave me pause long enough to think, *Maybe it isn't*, so I asked if I could go with them to see it. They cautioned me that it is actually a neighborhood—or "a ghetto" to the local Romanian citizens—an enclave solely for its residents, the people they call Gypsies.

The Roma are by choice a disenfranchised independent nation of people. They attorn to no authority and to no system of governance save their own. There are an estimated 621,000 of them living in Romania, out of the total of eleven million Roma living across Europe. Referred to as Roma by the Europeans, the Romanians call them *muste*, or flies. They're also called magnets because they deal in scrap metal—any metal for that matter— attached or unattached. For that reason and others, they are despised as a nuisance and a drain on Romania's budgets because they pay no income taxes.

Gary and Ken were two Americans who had felt led to Romania to start churches, which they did independently of each other. The Romanians would say Gary started a Gypsy church. Gary always said "No, a church for Romanians." They drove me and a friend to the palace to see it and pay a visit to some leaders in Gary's church. As we drove into the neighborhood, I was drawn to the sight of a man on crutches who was obviously laboring and in pain from his efforts. It was hot. I heard a whisper, "Make note of that man, you will see him again."

We parked in front of the neighborhood's namesake and got out of the car, preparing ourselves to go in. The iconic palace is an empty four-story building that was intended to be a block of flats, but it was left unfinished. Its slum-like appearance lent its derogatory identity to the entire neighborhood. The building itself is unlivable—even though it is occupied by scores of people. Its only utility is water, which runs in streams throughout the building. The water runs down to the floor below from the floor above, and ultimately it empties out of the building onto the street. The building has no other improvements. It's an empty shell: I saw no electricity, no lights, no heat, no toilets, no doors.

Like in most poor neighborhood settings, the men stood off together, watching us, almost hidden in between other buildings. As we got out of the car, they emerged to check us out, but seeing Gary and Ken, they moved back into the shadows. I walked into the building slowly and uninhibited. I walked up the stairs to each floor. Peering around the corners of empty doorways, I saw only the faces of the poorest Gypsy families inhabiting the bare concrete rooms. Generally, the rooms had mattresses and small gasoline stoves. I saw only women and small children. It was the small children who came out to see me first. I knelt down and spoke some brief phrases in Romanian, and they responded by taking my hand and walking me to their rooms. I did not go inside. The younger mothers were furtive and shy; most of them appeared to be in their teens. The older women were more brazen and unwelcoming. We didn't stay long. When we left, the men were there to say something I couldn't understand, then we got back in the car and drove to the home of Gary's parishioner.

Ken, Gary, my friend, and I, along with two men from Gary's church, were conversing quietly in the man's home. Without any warning, the door burst open, and two men carrying the man on crutches we'd passed on the street rushed into the room, all the while crying out, "It's the Americans. They're here and they will heal you." They had left his crutches outside the room, so they sat the man next to me on the couch. I saw the image of the paralyzed man being lowered by his friends through the roof of another home, this one in Capernaum, to be healed by Jesus.

The man sitting next to me was a large man; he would've been difficult for his friends to carry. He was hot from his exertion, and he seemed distraught while sobbing in Romanian for help. Glancing around the room, I waited for our hosts or for Gary or Ken to speak. But everyone was quiet, all of us stunned by the sudden intrusion and uncertain of what to do next.

I put my left arm around his shoulders and leaned in to whisper to the man.

"Do you know that God loves you?"

"Yes," he said.

"And do you know that I love you?" He looked at me and, with tears, nodded and said, "Yes, I know you love me."

We nodded to each other for a moment. "Then go in peace, brother, assured of the Father's love for you."

Throughout that brief exchange, the room was quiet—no one else had said a word. I'm not sure if the man and I spoke to each other in English or Romanian. But he spoke no English, and I couldn't have spoken my words to him in anything but English. He stood up and, with help from his friends, walked out of the room.

As we walked to the car to leave, my friend from home leaned into me and said, "You really do love these people, don't you?"

"Yes, I do love them."

Where do the words we speak originate? Do they just emerge?

Just now, at this moment, as I compose these recollections, for the first time I am aware that they were almost word for word the same words I'd whispered to the little boy in the hospital. And as I think on this, I'm reminded that I went looking for the suffering I knew I would find in the hospital. The same can be said for why I wanted to see the palace in Constanta and the Palace of the People. I hadn't known how or with whom suffering would manifest itself in any of these venues, but I could count on the absolute truth that suffering can be found everywhere and the same love that I have for my Father would want to touch it.

CHAPTER 17

You're Just Beginning

Whoever forces you to go one mile, go with him two.

—Matthew 5:41

Shortly after the man in the NGO director's office made his phone call, someone at the Constanta hospital agreed to lease me the PC#3 building and negotiate an agreement to care for the kids. I'm attempting to put into words the impact the hospital's willingness to find a mutual understanding had on my heart and my emotions. For five years, I had doggedly pursued a goal built on my hope that someone else would improve the kids' quality of life and take responsibility for their futures. I felt it was my role to facilitate that opportunity for Adi because I lived six thousand miles away, but I was willing to support the cost for him to author a program. It now appeared that the responsibility was shifting to me, but none of the pieces that were needed to transform the children's lives were yet in place. They were out there waiting to be gathered up, but I only saw a road stretched out in front of me with no end in sight. I was exhausted, and I wanted to stop—I had had enough of this crucible.

I asked Bob and Adi if they could complete an operating agreement and a lease on the PC#3 building and do it quickly, because I feared that the opportunity would be taken away from us should someone at the hospital come to their senses and realize what they'd agreed to do. I felt lacking in the stamina to contend with a long-term obligation to the kids and the care staff at PC#3 without terms and conditions in the agreements that would bind the hospital (whose building it was) or the doctor (who managed the medical care). We'd been given an opening and we had to move on it, but I had reached the limits of my emotional endurance.

I had stood frozen before the front door in 1992, fearful of entering as the evil poured out over me in a foul-smelling fog. In 1996, evil mocked me again as I fumed in Adi's car after being threatened by someone from behind the locked door. Now, by God's hand, the door stood open again, and yet again I stood frozen. There it was, the prize I wanted, but my lifelong fear of success flared. Having reached this moment of triumph, evil was calling me out, claiming that my desire to redeem PC#3 came out of a misbegotten sense of ethnocentric indignation. I was having to grow up again and, as God's man now, walk confidently into the darkness.

But this was no time for self-examination or procrastination. Not acting would continue the suffering and further the staff's skepticism that another curious visitor with good intentions would follow through. The day before I left to go home, I brought up the matter with Adi and told him I was finished, burnt out. I couldn't go on because my part of the work was done. I wanted him to say we'd brought the project to the place where he could take over now, but instead he said, "Hud, you can't quit now—you're just beginning." Later that same day, he repeated it at the airport as he dropped me off. "Hud, you can't quit now, you've just started. God's given these children to you. They're yours now."

Oh, how good it felt to get on that Swiss Air jet and get away from there, to escape back to the order and calm of Zurich to settle myself and listen to the Spirit for what was to come. I went home and waited to be led.

Adi and Bob continued their negotiations while I was away, and I joined them when I returned a few weeks later. At that point we only had a verbal agreement—more of a truce with the doctor than anything else—but the important thing was that it gave each of us what we wanted. I committed to pay for and manage the program of care for the kids. My commitment wasn't only to support a budget. I was committing myself to supporting the kids and the staff that was needed to care for the kids until there was no further need to do so. I was committing myself to the role of a father. I had seen when, in frustration, other NGOs had left their programs. Our staff had seen the others leave too. If I promised to support the staff, would they believe me? I wanted us to be different than the others.

The doctor and her foundation could continue their HIV research, absent the overhead that came with the care of the kids and the building. I felt it was better not to define how we would integrate our schedule of activities with the hospital's schedule of medical testing and experiments, something they wanted.

Prior to our being in place in PC#3 to enforce our rules, the doctor had unrestricted access to the kids. She could come and go as she pleased, sending orderlies over to PC#3 in hospital vans and snatching the kids up to bring them back to the hospital to do her testing and experiments. Going to the hospital was traumatic for the kids. The kids and their caregivers never knew when orderlies would rush in and, without asking, grab some kids—usually holding them under their arms kicking and screaming—then drive off to the infectious disease ward for shots and treatments with no explanation. Later, when the kids were ours, they would refuse to get into our van to go on an outing for a pizza or a trip to the park. You could read their expressions: "I'm not getting in there!" For some of them, it would be several years before they would get in a car to leave the house with staff.

Do you recall the fable of an ambitious and covetous camel, who on a cold desert night eventually moved into his owner's tent an inch at a time? Having entered into negotiations with the doctor and the hospital, I had won the opportunity I wanted by being patient. But I had won nothing unless I acted on the opportunity and perfected it, because nothing about this mission was static. Every part of it was in motion. The parts needed to be gathered up quickly now and fit together before the other parties to the negotiations came to their senses and realized what they had given up. I don't mean to say we needed to create a perfect project; as a servant I needed to wait for my instructions and then live them out, trusting my Master to bring to me the resources to accomplish them.

Romania is a country of people tacitly respectful of being a regulated populace. People's relations with a government agency are spelled out in documents, and no document is recognized as official and enforceable unless it is stamped in red ink with the registered and licensed seal of the authorized gatekeeper and their agency. Their documents are as numerous as the leaves on the trees, and they regulate life in exquisite details that they deem logical. It can be humorous. (For example, to apply for or renew your driver's license, you must declare your gender and prove it by undergoing an inspection of your genitals by a doctor or nurse.) But then like the leaves, their documents eventually curl up and blow away, to be replaced with more documents reflecting whatever new regulations have been enacted by whatever agency has the authority to do so.

Knowing that, I wanted no part in a clearly defined care document spelling out in detail the terms of our mutual obligations. This allowed me to hide my intentions for the kids' futures. Asking the doctor for a new, detailed, mutually-shared system of care (on which they would never follow through) would have been a tacit admission that she still had authority over the kids' lives. I wanted that taken away from her. Had she and the hospital asked for my intentions, I would have said, "As long as your medical experiments don't conflict with our daily schedules, and if you ask first before coming to the house to pick up the kids, and one of our staff goes with the kids, you're welcome to come and visit." That restriction on the doctor's intrusions eventually came to pass, but only an inch at a time.

Cultural differences were obstacles to problem solving. For example, start with the need for an American foundation to manage the lives of the kids. My friends in Romania were puzzled by my skepticism that their hospital administration lacked the motivation to reform itself. The avoidance behavior that Romanian nationalism rationalizes made it easier for my friends to assume that people in positions of authority in the hospital system would want to improve conditions in their orphanages. My friends believed our intervention wasn't necessary. Some called it presumptuous, even arrogant. They would say, "Why are you so angry? The government will fix the problem." My rejoinder to that was "Why would they do that? They created the problem. Why would they now spend their own money to fix it when the children's suffering generates revenue for them?" But if my friends were right and the system ever did come to its senses and reform itself, our kids would be dead by the time the reforms filtered down to them. I wouldn't risk that possibility.

As the expression goes, when parties agree to agree to terms that will eventually bind them, time is of the essence. I needed to complete an operating and leasehold agreement for the building between the entity the hospital chose to represent them as lessor and me as a not-for-profit corporation as lessee, formed within the legal framework of the laws of Romania. The American foundation I formed, working in Romania with an American majority serving on its board, would lease the building, physically occupying it and providing it with a staff of Romanians that we had selected and trained to manage the care of the children.

I would also need to form a not-for-profit foundation in the US, most likely a 501(c)(3) corporation to allow us to collect tax-deductible funds to support the work. I'd need a board. I needed to create a realistic budget out of more than unsubstantiated guesses and my imagination to care for the kids and staff. We also needed an in-country director to manage the house and its staff, someone who could communicate in English with us in the US. The duration of the commitment didn't matter. For better or for worse, we were going to be there as long as God permitted us to stay if we could just get there and get started. My hope for the outcome of our efforts was that once we were in place, some of the sicker children could at least die with some dignity in the company of people who loved them. We thought most of them wouldn't last more than two years after we took over, and I didn't want their deaths to come before we could get there.

Then came the second most important decision I made after agreeing to obey the call to go to Romania. The lease required a foundation registered in Romania to act as the lessee of the hospital's building (PC#3). To save the time it would take to petition a court to allow us to form a stand-alone US Chi Ro Romania foundation, Adi suggested we use his Osana Foundation to act as the Romanian foundation. Osana, and not an American foundation, would receive funds from the US to create and manage the budget, set the vision of the work, and manage the mission with the Romanian staff. The US contingent would provide the funds through its own stand-alone US foundation. To suborn ourselves to Adi's Osana Foundation would have taken less time and been less complicated to manage, but the Spirit whispered to not use that vehicle.

I wanted our US foundation to direct the activities of the kids' lives, following Marolen's model of arranging the kids into small families under the constant watch of two mamas. That meant the staff would operate though Chi Ro Romania, a US foundation. The Romanian management model is vertical; every decision runs downhill from one person, from the top down to the lowest members of the staff. Only one person has the authority to respond, adapt, and act. In a houseful of special needs kids, the only way they knew how to keep order was by tyrannical neglect and abuse. That was PC#3's model, not Marolen's, and the old model needed to be discarded. This decision to form our own foundation was the nexus for everything else that has followed since then.

But forget all that organizational chart stuff. If it isn't true that people's beliefs, values, and morals shape their decisions, consider this: here we were with a house full of human beings, most of them sick and helpless special needs children whom their culture considered castoffs. Could I rely on local management to discard their conventional wisdom and risk sending checks to preserve the status quo? That would be like partnering with the doctor if Adi ever left, and that made no sense. And the Spirit's whisper also cautioned me that it was safer to form a new and independent US foundation and direct it for another reason—I accepted that while corruption was unlikely, it was still possible. In an environment where there is a paucity of resources, temptation can be too strong for a soul, and resentment of a seemingly bottomless funding source leading to corruption is inevitable. It took more time to form our own American foundation in Romania, but that decision proved to be wise.

CHAPTER 18

Opening Day and the Weekend Before

Shepherd Your people … the flock of Your possession …
I will show you miracles.

—Micah 7:14, 15

On Monday, June 1, 1998, the body of Christ walked through the front door of PC#3 unimpeded, and at that moment PC#3 passed away and a House of New Life (in Christ) emerged from the darkness. The building's new name isn't an original; there are hundreds of Houses of New Life all around the world, and most of them are focused on the common theme of restoring life to a soul. In our case, our caregivers went looking for children to help them find a new life—their new life—the life the society all around them claimed didn't exist.

For the children still living there, the effects of their neglect did not go away quickly or quietly, and as you might expect, they never have. But that day, when their new life began, there was no one to stop our first director at CVN and her team from entering the building. They had statutory authority to do so, but even if they hadn't, her team could have walked in without hindrance:

there was no one there except the thirty-six children, left alone and unattended for the weekend. The Romanian staff had just walked away Friday afternoon at the end of their shift and had not told us that the children would be left alone until we arrived Monday morning. I was not there to witness the hell the former caregivers had left behind.

My fears had always been for the safety of the children once my intentions of supplanting the doctor's regime were made public. My fear was proven well-founded. Starting at the beginning of negotiations for the lease and then in the days leading up to the June 1 start date, the children's suffering steadily increased. The basics of care, food, the few medicines they shared from the hospital dispensary, laundry, human touch and nurture, fresh water for hygiene, and food preparation—plus certain cosmetically attractive kids—began to disappear from PC#3. Some kids died, others were taken to the doctor's other homes and replaced with her problem children. It became a race to get there while the ones well enough to stay alive could be helped.

In some cases, we were, in fact, too late. The child I feared was getting close to death was gone. Ribana had been a beautiful, cheerful little girl. Even in her suffering as HIV wore her down, her demeanor was always cheerful. That Monday morning, they found her dead.

This was the lowest point that could be reached. What our team found was a chaos akin to a *Lord of the Flies* scenario, which I still find unimaginable. Adi came shortly afterwards, when the director called him for help. He brought a video camera to record the criminal conditions. He also brought a pump, borrowed from a friend at the church.

The pump was used to clear the sewage and filth out of the basement, but as soon as it was pumped out, it flowed back in.

The video shows the walls of the building smeared with feces and puddles of urine on the floors. The toilets couldn't be flushed; the water had been turned off. The children had been drinking out of the toilets before the water ran out, and they were now dehydrated. They had been scavenging for food remnants and Froot Loops left on the floors. The weather was hot; the house was like an oven. They said the noise was demonic, and the smell … I don't know what to say about the smell. I wasn't there that day, but I've written earlier that the odor from the place came home in my clothing.

We didn't expect—we could not have conceived of—such a cruel transition from the hospital's team. There was no "hand off" of the kids from one caring soul to the next as you might expect from professional people charged with the responsibility of caring for helpless lives. They just walked out Friday afternoon and left the kids behind. We didn't imagine people could do such cruel things. Maybe they thought they were spiting us by leaving behind such monstrous conditions—I don't know. They left us with nothing in the house to clean up with. Our team had to walk over the feces and mess just to assess the damage, and all the while the children's chaos from hunger and fear was exploding all around them. There was no water, hot or cold. There were no buckets or disinfectant. Most of the bathroom sinks and toilets had been removed by the staff for use in the doctor's other houses. Our team sent some of our staff out to buy buckets and gallons of bleach, and they went to work cleaning it up.

There was more than enough cloth to clean with. The clothing the kids were wearing were mere rags, and those that had been donated to replace what they wore were found piled in a big stack in one room. The good clothing had been stolen by the former staff. Dirty clothing lay piled in another big stack in the room described as a laundry. Some of the girls turned out to be boys. It was easy to be confused because of the length of their hair and the dresses they wore. Those kids who could dress themselves simply put on whatever they could find. Dresses or pants, it didn't matter to them.

This picture makes the larger point—that of the hospital system's view of these children. To those in the system, the individual dignity of these castoffs meant nothing. To those in authority charged with their care, it was better that the kids did not live. It was easier to lose them in the numbers of an unfunded budget and eliminate the problem of the authority's culpability for permitting such a hell under their watch should any kind of an "audit" question their neglect. An audit wasn't going to originate from Romanians. Many of the kids didn't even have birth certificates. They were from the poorer families, or worse for them, they were Roma kids. To the State, those kids didn't warrant the trouble to create a record of their existence. It was less work to discard them than to prove they existed. If they remained alive, they were expensive liabilities.

I was aware of this mindset on the part of the system before that first day. I'd seen the effects of it in the absence of care in the pediatric wards of the infectious disease hospital and PC#3. I blame myself for not being better prepared and for not being there to share the work. It was not just a lack of supplies to clean with; it was also not preparing our staff with greater vehemence for the chaos that would fall on them once they returned to the building. I was in attendance during a few early orientation meetings with Marolen and her staff at Casa Speranta. It was obvious to me that our staff was not allowing the severity of the circumstances Marolen cautioned them about to sink in.

I spoke with our "mamas" at one of the orientation meetings

at Casa Speranta. I apologized and warned them that the years of neglect and abuse the children had lived with since infancy were going to explode in uncontrollable anger. "You're changing their world," I explained, "and they're not going to like it. It will feel to them as if they've lost control. You are going to have to be the rock upon which their anger falls like a huge wave. And it will break on you and break and break again, and you cannot respond as the others have before and as they want you to. If you do, the children will never learn to trust another human or learn from you that they are loved unconditionally. When they begin to learn that you know why they're angry, and that they are loved no matter what, they will begin to know the love of the Father. However, that is perceived by whatever cognitive ability each individual child has. They are individuals, not nameless faceless numbers. They are each a child of God. For them to know that, that's why we are here."

I was too hard on myself and the staff. The building was a place utterly unsuitable for pets, let alone sick children. The remodeling schedule was still in process, the start date not yet determined. The interface with Marolen's team from Casa Speranta was not going well. We were asking our staff, who were unskilled and untrained in remediating the effects of very sick kids with special needs and Reactive Detachment Disorder, to bear the brunt of the children's anger.

I hoped for too much too soon. But the truth is none of us knew how much time we'd have with the children because they were so sick. It was a shock to walk into the house and find one child already dead. All you had to do was look around at the rest of the children and question their resolve to keep living. But these children were survivors. They were the tough ones. But when a sponsor asked me during a meeting at our home, "So, Hud, what's next? What do you expect will happen to these kids?" I had to answer: "Kirt, I have no idea. I expect the kids may live another two years and then die. In that time, I hope we are able to convey to them how much they are loved, but compared to what they've had to live through, that should be enough."

Below is a complete list of the names of the children we found living in PC#3 the day it became the House of New Life. Most of the kids I had gotten to know during my earlier visits were gone to other settings. A few were still there though. It includes a partial description (as written by the Romanian staff at the time) of their physical and developmental issues, although the diagnoses were superficial and inexpert. The children's individual medical records were incomplete, if they existed at all. As time has passed, our staff has been able (with the help of some more thoughtful local physicians as well as expatriate medical, developmental, and dental professionals) to know more about the children's condition. Just living with the children and getting to know them over the years has revealed more special needs issues and has been the burden of the teams who have cared for them. We consider our staff to be saints.

These are the ones we found God sharing His company with. Truly, the least of the least …

1. *Georgetta* (Female. 9 years, HIV-positive)
2. *Florin* (Male. 9 years, serious encephalopathy, HIV-positive, does not speak, does not feed himself, no social skills, is often agitated, walks only with assistance and with difficulty)
3. *Vasilica* (Female. 8 years, HIV-positive, does not eat without assistance, does not speak, does not go to the toilet alone)

4. *Bumba* (Male. 10 years, encephalopathy, HIV-positive, reduced sociability)
5. *Selda* (Female. 10 years, HIV-positive)
6. *Alin* (Male. 10 years old, HIV-positive, encephalopathy, heart valve issues undiagnosed)
7. *Deda* (Female. 9 years, HIV-positive)
8. *Titus* (Male. 11 years, HIV-positive, unintelligible speech patterns, rigid left leg makes movement difficult)
9. *Tanure* (Female. 10 years, HIV-positive)
10 *Ionela* (Female. 11 years, encephalopathy, HIV-positive, ophthalmological problems, problems with her feet and legs, walks, speech problems)
11. *Emilea-Elena* (Female. 12 years, HIV-positive)
12. *Claudia* (Female. 10 years, HIV-positive)
13. *Florin* (Male. 11 years, HIV-positive, does not speak, does not eat on his own, difficulty walking)
14. *Antoneta* (Female. 9 years, HIV-positive)
15. *Ribana Grancea* (Female. 9 years, deceased 6/1/98)
16 Laura (Female. 11 years, HIV-positive, hepatitis undiagnosed)
17. *Nicolae* (Male. HIV-positive, nocturnal enuresis)
18. *Sabrie* (Female. 10 years, HIV-positive)
19. *Alina* (Female. 10 years, HIV-positive, foot/leg problems make walking difficult, reduced social skills)
20. *Cornelius* (Male. 9 years, serious advanced encephalopathy, HIV-positive, easily irritable, aggressive anger, partial loss of sphincter control)
21. *Vasilica* (Female. 10 years, ophthalmological problems)
22. *Giorgiana* (Female. 10 years. HIV-positive, does not speak at all, nocturnal enuresis, reduced social skills)
23. *Suzana* (Female. 11 years, HIV-positive, enuresis, easily irritable and aggressive)

24. *Petronela* (Female. 10 years, HIV-positive, does not speak, does not eat on her own)
25. *Ferdi* (Male, 10 years. advanced grave encephalopathy, HIV-positive, does not speak, often agitated and aggressive)
26. *Velentina* (Female. 8 years, HIV-positive)
27. *Ancuta* (Female. 10 years, HIV-positive)
28. *Crina* (Female. 9 years, HIV-positive, does not speak, does not eat on her own)
29. *Stefan* (Male. 9 years, HIV-positive)
30. *Maria* (Female. 10 years, HIV-positive)
31. *Sevima* (Female. 11 years, HIV-positive)
32. *Narcis* (Female. 10 years, HIV-positive)
33. *Maria* (Female. 9 years, HIV-positive, does not eat without assistance, does not speak, does not go to the toilet alone)
34. *Adrian* (Male. 10 years, HIV-positive, ophthalmological problems)
35. *Florentina* (Female. 9 years, HIV-positive, congenital malformation of one of her legs)
36. *Constantin* (Male. 9 years, HIV-positive, nocturnal enuresis)

In the years following my early visits, I'd had a few sharp exchanges with customs agents, border police, hospital nurses, and Roma on the street. The first serious confrontations took place on my visits to the infectious disease hospital wards, but of all the challenges, none were more frightening than my confrontations with the presence of evil. But now that we had taken possession of PC#3, evil loomed as a wave on the horizon to sweep us away. When we renamed PC#3 the House of New

Life, meaning new life in Christ, evil openly flaunted its authority over the children, knowing we went in the name of Christ.

Because of what the kids had lived and the wounds they carried, evil was reflected back to me through their eyes and voices. To reach their hearts, I would look into a child's eyes to see what would be returned. My expression of invitation was often reflected back to me in their eyes with an odd flickering light. Sometimes their light was a combination of anger, disdain, hatred, or vacancy when their souls were in a fog and they wanted to be invisible. Or they would yell at me, answering the eyes of my heart with an unearthly screeching sound sent through bared teeth and backed by a hateful glare. I saw evil in their eyes and heard it in the lies of some of the people who had cared for the kids. These were the former staff who personally benefitted from the kids' misery, adding to it by providing pedophiles access to the kids or outright stealing donations of money and gifts in kind. You know it's evil when you see someone subjugating another for profit.

This was my experience. Evil challenges you—at times it even spits in your face. Evil knows you are the body of Christ, so it tests and challenges you and curses you with the words: *So, what are you going to do about this, weakling? You want to come in here and see if you can handle what goes on here, see if you can handle what I have for you? This is my place; these children belong to me. Don't waste your time here.*

I would stand my ground. *You have no authority over me, Satan. I am coming after you, and I am going to redeem what belongs to me! These are my children! I'm going to plant the light of Christ in this place and drive you out in the name of Jesus!*

How are you going to do that, weakling?

I'm going to pray God gives me what belongs to Him, and I'm going to keep coming back, and each time I come it will be in the name of Jesus.

Others will see that, join me, and drive you out. The kids will know the love of the Father, and God will be glorified.

These words of challenge I exchanged in my soul. I did not speak them out loud to anyone, and I have not asked anyone else if they, too, heard and returned Satan's challenge. Though my countenance remained implacable, inside my soul there raged a terrible indignation! But evil was defeated, and I watched, whether tearfully or calmly with peace, as God gathered His children unto Himself.

Earlier in the narrative I spoke of my habit of standing quietly against a wall, watching the routine activities going on all around me. For a 6'2" American to remain unobtrusive in a setting like that isn't easy, but if I remained still, it was possible to blend in and not be noticed. Alone in my thoughts one afternoon, I was interrupted when I looked down to see Adi Secure come stand next to me, take my finger, and hold it for most of an hour until I left. He never said a word.

Some months later, at a presentation at the Holy Trinity Baptist Church, we were trying to encourage more volunteers from the church to help with the needs ongoing. The son of one of the church elders had been going as a youth volunteer and he shared in a church service his experience of Adi Secure simply walking up to him and holding his finger like he did mine. Describing his experience, the young man said one of the most memorable things any of us have heard coming out of the experience of going into PC#3. He said: "When I was encouraged to go there and help, I didn't know what I could do. What can I do? I'm an accounting student. What skills do I have that can contribute to these children's welfare? While I was just standing around one day, a little boy walked up to me and took my finger and held it for a long time, and I realized all he needed from me was my company and my finger. So I ask you, how many of us cannot afford to give just one finger?"

Adi Secure was one of the "survivors." It seemed no matter what was thrown at the survivors, they good-naturedly took it and chose to live. But when they had had enough of life, you could look into their eyes and see a different light, and you knew they had surrendered to their disease and the loneliness. I saw that same look in Adi's eyes shortly before he died.

Thus, the eyes of the children didn't always reflect evil's wounding. There were times when their eyes were soft, receptive, tired, hungry for love, hungry for the opportunity of self-expression, or simply tearfully joy-filled, like the day Maria was given her first ever birthday party—the first birthday party ever given to just one single child at PC#3 (now the House of New Life). On the actual day of her birthday, all the kids who could be were seated around the big table in the upstairs family room. The practice had been to celebrate on one day all the kids whose birthdays fell during that month. So here they were, all sitting around with little paper hats expecting the usual group party, and in walked Maria's mama with a cake and candles with her name in the icing. Maria was seated at the head of the table wearing the crown of a queen. Her mama placed the cake in front of her, and while we all sang her name to the Romanian birthday song, she burst into tears! Now all the kids and their mamas started crying, and I was crying too. Celebrating each child's birthday became the practice from then on, and nobody was ever unhappy again at a birthday party in the House of New Life.

CHAPTER 19

NATO's Grant

But seek first His kingdom and His righteousness ... and all
these things will be provided to you.

—Matthew 6:33

While Adi and Bob were perfecting the lease agreement, I was in California taking care of my American life. One day, the phone rang. It was Marolen, calling from Romania. "Guess what I have for you! I have $115,000 from NATO to fix up your building! I got ahold of the American naval attaché in Bucharest, and he applied in Chi Rho's name for these funds. He said that every year NATO forces have excess operating funds that they don't use. Some group of Marines somewhere figures out where grants should go to deserving folks, and they give out money for outreach in NATO member countries. It's been approved for you to use to repair your building. Isn't that cool?"

"Cool? Are you kidding!? That's very generous, Marolen. Why didn't you get it for your place?"

"Well, I think you have a bigger problem with that building of yours than we do in ours. I just wanted to help you to get started."

She was right.

Where to begin? We had jumped into our House of New Life (Casa Viata Noua/CVN) with both feet, and we had landed in a big hole.

Here's a short lesson in pre-revolutionary Romanian construction to explain the size of that hole. With the exception of the artisan homes and buildings of the elites, during the Communist era all the buildings were constructed from blocks cut from hardened concrete foam. The building blocks were held together with plaster and stucco, steel reinforcing bars, and mortar. The plumbing for water and sewage and the electrical systems were attached to the walls and ceilings with brackets. For the PC#3 building to become habitable, the walls and ceilings would have to be stripped down to the bare surfaces and the crumbling and corroded electrical conduit and plumbing replaced. New sinks and toilets were needed to replace the units stolen by the former staff and the broken ones that remained, and those new units reattached to the reinstalled plumbing lines. New electrical outlets and lights would also need to be connected, the heating radiators replaced, and new ones connected to a new diesel-fueled heating system in the basement, which needed to be pumped out because it was permanently flooded with sewage from the street and CVN. To keep the sewage from flowing back into the basement, the sewer lateral to the street from the building would need to be torn out and reinstalled to create the proper fall in elevation for the waste to flow out of the building.

But how to care for sick children, most with profound special needs and already in shock from the abrupt changes in their routines, while you rebuild a building around them with nothing to support their bodily needs? They would have to live somewhere else while the building was being rebuilt. And winter was approaching.

While I had been wondering how much it would take, and my estimates for funding the costs were just a guess, Marolen had been collaborating with the naval attaché to arrange a grant to fund the cost of rebuilding CVN in its entirety. I had thought if we could raise at least $75,000 to provide some heat and electricity, the rest would come later. If they had not acted, I don't know when I would have been able to find the money to do the work.

I asked Marolen how to gain access to the funds. She didn't know. "You'll have to call the attaché and ask him. He'll explain it to you. Have fun! See you when you get over here." Click. She was gone. Cell phones and internet coverage weren't there yet, and calls were expensive.

I phoned the attaché in Bucharest, and he explained, "You'll have to meet the facilities guys at the American embassy and present your plans." He cautioned me that if Adi, as a lone Romanian, approached the embassy to collect the money, the release of the funds would never happen. He gave me the name of the embassy staffer to contact to get the funds released and start the work. Now that we had the funds, we thought our troubles were over and the whole thing would be a piece of cake. So I got back on the plane to Constanta in the spring of 1998.

The process of releasing the funds, however, was not what I'd imagined. Throughout the process, and even after the building was completed, I had to prove repeatedly to auditors sent by the embassy that I was not embezzling or laundering funds through Romanian contacts. It never occurred to me that the embassy staff would see us as nuisances and possibly frauds. Not expecting any of this beforehand, we called on the embassy with an appointment to meet Mike, a general services officer.

Even though it takes four hours on the old two-lane road, we drove from Constanta to Bucharest in the heat and humidity of summer 1998 rather than taking the train. We needed Adi's car to get around in the city. Once in Bucharest, the real driving begins. Cars, together with trucks belching diesel smoke and exhaust, are like corpuscles in the capillaries being squeezed along, rubbing up against each other as the drivers honk and push to gain some perceived advantage. From the outskirts we made our way through the chaos and found a place to park near the embassy, then we walked the rest of the way. Like most embassies, the American embassy isn't hospitable until you get inside the gates. I explained to the Marines at the gate that we had a meeting with Mike. They rang inside, and we waited. We stood at the front gate and waited another thirty minutes before we were ushered into an air-conditioned receiving room just inside the gates. Mike met us with Peter, another embassy staffer. They were clearly annoyed at the disruption and were unashamed to show it. I was expecting another kind of reception, maybe even kudos from a fellow American congratulating another American for showing up trying to make a difference in a difficult place to work for some underprivileged kids. Wasn't that why we were all there in Romania, to serve the greater good? I thought he'd applaud a fellow citizen's initiative and be eager to help us.

There was a brief introduction, then the question, "What's this all about?"

In gracious real estate developer tone, I schmoozed. "Hi, Mike. I'm Hud Staffield, and this is my partner, Adi. We've taken over an orphanage in Constanta. I'm told by the naval attaché that you're holding some NATO funds designated for our use to rebuild the orphanage, and we'd like to collect those funds. I think you know that."

"I hope you don't expect me to go to Constanta to supervise this project."

I should've been shocked, but at the moment I was relieved to hear that option. I didn't want the interference. "Oh no, we don't expect you to have to do that. We're going to do it. We'll do the work. I was told I needed to contact you to get the funds released."

"Well, I'm sorry, but I don't have time to help you with this project. Do you know how many light bulbs I have to change every day in the embassy facilities? And there are other responsibilities I have: air conditioning problems, windows and doors to repair or replace. These are all old buildings, and I have construction projects of my own. I don't have time to do a construction project in Constanta."

Our naval attaché had cautioned me earlier about the work ethic and attitudes of embassy staff regarding what staff considered distractions—and we were clearly a distraction. Before he became naval attaché to Romania, he had been a RIO, the Navy acronym for radar intercept officer. He had been a back seater doing his duty in Navy jets in the US fleet's naval operations. The military guys working in state department positions approached problem-solving with a definite "can do" attitude. The attaché's view of embassy support staff was that they took on new projects carefully. What Adi and I hadn't understood was that construction work with American funds had to be directed and the funding controlled by this same embassy staff to avoid the possibility of embezzlement.

Mike went on. "To release the funds and do the work yourselves, you'll need to prepare narrative plans and specs for us to review and approve, and you will prepare a budget with verifiable estimates to match the work you propose doing. You'll need working drawings and bids from your subs. You'll need to submit all this to us for review and approval, then you will pass a JAG review by a NATO architectural review staffer based out of

London. We will make progress payments every thirty days, and upon completion, retention will be released after an auditor from the embassy signs off that the preapproved specifications have been completed 100 percent."

I contemplated what I had just heard, reflecting on its consequences to us. Nothing was static; everything was in motion. How to pull this all together? Which of the original kids would be left alive by the time we finished jumping through all these hoops? How could I get working drawings done and approved by these guys and settle their concerns in so little time? Were they thinking of completing this project next year? Winter was perhaps seven months away. No one trusted anything or anyone. The embassy staff needed to know that I was not going away, that they would have to let us do the work and they would supervise it, but I would make it easy for them. Our conversation continued but with a greater sense of urgency.

"Mike, look at me. I have brown eyes and brown hair. I am an American citizen, and I have come a long way from California to see you. I am a US citizen standing here at the US embassy with a real problem, and I know how to solve it. I am a commercial real estate developer. I have built, leased, and managed over 1.5 million square feet of buildings in the United States. This is Adi. He is a civil engineer and a general contractor. We know how to do this. We need you to release the funds that belong to us so that we can complete the renovation of an orphanage building before winter. Those kids are sick, Mike. They do not have heating and air-conditioning problems or light bulbs to change. They don't even have enough electricity for laundry, let alone heating and air conditioning. So, Mike, what do you need us to do to help you do your job?"

There was the key to the grant money standing right in front of me, money we needed to refurbish the building—money that belonged to us—and we couldn't get it. And there was something else we needed that the embassy couldn't help us with. We needed to pay for operating the house every year, and I didn't know where to go to get that. I thought, *I have to get started finding operating cash right now because grants take a long time to perfect. We don't have a lot of time. Who do I go to, where do I go?* Like a loan application for a development project, I thought, who's in the market for funding the operating expenses of orphanages in Romania?

It was a simple prayer: *Where do I go to find the resources to do this? Grants take a lot of time. Who wants to help me fund this?*

The answer came as a whisper, *You have it.*

I wasn't sure I'd heard what I thought I'd heard. *What? What was that?*

Louder now the whisper came. *You have it.*

And in an instant, He allowed me to see my entire life up to that moment to fully appreciate the truth of His words. As if looking down a tunnel, I was able to see the people, the events, the opportunities, and failures and successes of my life in progression, stretching all the way back from a childhood moment at my grandmother's breakfast table.

At my grandmother's house in Arizona, my favorite part of the day had been waking and hearing the ticking of the clock in the living room. It was a steady metronome of stability. Apart from my grandmother, it was the heart of the house, and her house was the safest place in my world.

The fireplace under the clock in the living room gave off the scent of cottonwood smoke and, with it, the expectation of warmth. From the kitchen would come more smells: bacon, biscuits, homemade syrup, and waffles. The soft, snowy-haired woman would reach for me with a smile, her face announcing her pleasure at my presence—then at last the unconditional embrace.

The breakfast table was my grandmother's time to be alone with me and my brother and sister. Being with her was easy. I wanted to be with her. There was always enough to eat, and she made us anything we wanted. Later in life I would appreciate the method of her lessons, but as a child I only felt her warmth. So, when she began to speak at the breakfast table, I always listened carefully. She told us family stories, and she spoke of the talents, a Samaritan, and the other parables. She spoke of a gift. "Should anything come to you, don't squander the gift on things that don't last," she said. "If you spend it, it's gone. Invest it, and the gift will multiply and care for you with enough left over to care for others."

As she spoke, I stopped listening and allowed my thoughts to drift away. Gifts like the ones she spoke of—these imaginary gifts that lifted their recipients into lives with choices and privilege—only came to fictional characters in stories or novels, like *The Count of Monte Cristo* or *Treasure Island*.

Don't live with expectations from dreams, I told myself. *Still, what if that might happen to me? I've always been able to trust her. What if a gift became a reality, and one day I did receive a gift of some money? How would I invest it to make it work for me? Will I have the ability to seize the opportunity? What if it's the wrong opportunity and I lose the gift? Wealth might protect me and give me control, privilege, self-respect, and respect from others, and most important … the safety that came with control. No one could hurt me; I'd be too powerful. This is worth hoping for but not counting on.* But my thoughts were interrupted by the words I'd been listening for. "Now go, you children. Have fun and don't slam the door!" At a run, we had flown out of her kitchen off the back porch steps, slamming the door in our haste to find the day's adventures.

A gift had come. My parents and my grandparents had begun a ranching operation when I was a small boy. My grandmother insisted that a provision be included in the partnership agreement that a portion of the annual profits from the ranch's profits accrue to each of my parents' children. I was sixteen when the operation at the ranch terminated and I received the unexpected sum of money. Ten years later I used some of the money to buy land and build a building in what is now Silicon Valley. With a few other partners we developed commercial properties for the emerging electronic and semi-conductor industries that sprang up in Santa Clara County.

My grandmother had given me a gift; she sowed the seed of the parable of the Sower. Once removed, her hands would now comfort some children that would never know her. I can't wait to see her again to celebrate her trust in me.

In that moment of awareness, in the US Embassy in Bucharest, I felt overwhelming peace. There had been a purpose for everything. He had created me and shaped me to find those children in PC#3. I found Him among the children, His heart hidden in a field. I had been given what I needed to buy the field.

I answered, "I do. I have it."

Then I heard Him again. *There's something else I want you to see.*

There were my hands emerging from my heart stretched out in front of me holding something up. It was not the children, it was their pain, His pain, my pain. He said, *Hold it up.* And I said, *But what if no one comes? I'll be left holding it alone! It's too heavy for me.*

Do you trust Me?

Yes, I do.

Hold it up for people and people will be drawn to it, but only those who can see it will come.

CHAPTER 20

The Caregivers

She watches over the activities of her household,
And does not eat the bread of idleness.
Her children rise up and bless her ...

—Proverbs 31:27-28

That spring 1998 agreement with the doctor had allowed us to move into PC#3 on Monday, June 1. And with that, we had entered a netherworld of uncertainty. It was the waiting period that preyed upon my worst fears because the contract created a period during which the hospital could have reneged on its agreement and reversed the direction the lives of the kids were about to take. In a Romanian document, cause or intent is subject to the needs of the politician interpreting the provisions of the document. As my friend the secretary to the Constanta County council once explained to me, "I'm a lawyer, and documents are drafted by lawyers to be interpreted by other lawyers to allow for political means; hence the proliferation of documents."

While we waited for June 1 to arrive, we lacked four things to complete the transformation of PC#3 to a House of New Life.

First, we needed the kids and, along with them, the jurisdiction to care for them. What was a House of New Life with no kids? While we waited for the term of the lease to commence and the agreement to become binding, the doctor kept rearranging our cohort. The kids who had begun to trust us were being taken elsewhere, and others were brought in who heretofore were strangers to me. A close friend asked me, "The kids you eventually began with, did you choose them or did they choose you?" I couldn't answer him plainly. I shared a conversation with God that had taken place during those uncertain days. *These are not the kids I wanted.* It was the Spirit who said, *These are the children I've brought you.*

Second, we needed a staff of caregivers. While the staff waited for our contract to begin, each of them had to look to their futures. Where would they find work if we failed? They asked each other: "Who are these new people, and what commitment will they make to us? Can we depend on them? All the other foreign foundations have a history of coming and going, and our families depend on us working. It isn't legal for us to not have a job."

After that, we needed a home. The building we began with was unlivable. In its present state, the old PC#3 was barely a step above the "palace," that shell of an unfinished block of flats inhabited by the poorer Roma families of Constanta. As things stood, our caregivers would have to commit to caring for sick and angry children with none of the basics needed for providing nutrition and hygiene. I was able to say that we had a plan worked out with the NATO grant, but it was still just a promise until the work actually began. And while construction was underway, the kids would need to be moved to another place to live in the interim. These kinds of dramatic and rapid changes would result in stress placed on the kids, and their fearful outbursts would fall on the caregivers.

Finally, we needed trust—and confidence. As I think now, while I'm writing, the fourth necessity was as important as the other three. I believed God; I trusted Him. But I needed to convey that same trust and confidence to the staff that they should stay and share the love that they had always wanted to give the kids but had been constrained by workplace circumstances from sharing.

The most odious condition the doctor required under our agreement was that we pay for one of her nurses to be at the house every day "to supervise the kid's medical needs as they arose." It sounded reasonable during the negotiations, but the need to provide medical care was nonsense. If needs arose, the kids went to the hospital. What made it truly odious was the plan's design. The nurses assigned to us were there to be informants and sow distrust within our staff, trying to encourage them to leave us and go serve somewhere else. One of them in particular sat in the little clinic room and chain-smoked in a building crowded with sick children. As our staff went about their day's work, the informants whispered rumors to them: "You'll be fired when they occupy the building, and they will allow the children's body parts to be sold when they die." (Practices like that had gone on, though it was unimaginable to begin with when we considered the children's HIV status.) It was cruel manipulation, considering that a small core of the staff truly loved these kids. It was the love they felt that helped me overcome their doubts and those of the others from the distrust being sown.

I spoke earlier of confronting evil. Each time I visited, a few of them would whisper to me: "Is it true? Are we going to be fired when you have your own people here? You won't need us anymore. Are you going to get rid of the kids when they die and sell their organs as body parts for profits?"

"You are my people," I asked. "Who's telling you these things?"

All of the "plants" were, but it was their chief, the former director, who had locked Adi and me out, whom I confronted in the open so that our staff could see or hear that she had been challenged. I said to her, "If you have any personal dignity at all, you'll stop telling these lies or I'll have you removed."

She challenged me right back. "You don't scare me, and you can't remove me. I have a job when I leave here. I'm with the doctor's foundation."

"I know who you are and who you answer to. I want you to stop these lies."

Losing the staff was my greatest uncertainty in those days. I needed them. If they left fearing job security, we'd have to find and recruit a new group of people. Imagine trying to encourage a new, inexperienced recruit to come and work in the setting we were about to unleash. But more to the point, I wanted the old staff to stay and have a chance to work fulfilled, not disrespected and abused as they had been.

We kept the staff by keeping them engaged in our plans for the future. I consistently reinforced to them that positive change was coming—the opposite of what was being offered as rumors from their peers at other board and care settings. All of what they had been told about us had been negative. The big rock in a small pond was trashing the status quo. What we were promising was so uncharacteristic of anything they had lived with as children or experienced in their work careers. We told them we would offer them training and support. We described the Casa Speranta method of separating the children into families and told them that they would work in teams. The building would be rebuilt. There would be better food, a kitchen with new equipment, and care that came in the form of a laundry with washing machines. There would be heating in the building, hot water for washing, and clothing for the kids. We were actually recruiting them for jobs they already held.

Not all was rosy, however. After having seen some of them in action, I could imagine firing them. But we agreed it would be fair to allow any who chose to be interviewed and stay on to keep their jobs if they chose to undergo the job review. This, too, was unheard of in Romania: interviewing for a job? In the Communist State, you completed your training and they slotted you into the job you were trained to do. From then on you weren't supported or resourced, and you couldn't be fired, only transferred.

One woman in particular I looked forward to firing. I had seen her in action, and I thought I knew her feelings toward the kids. I'd seen the kids bait her while she did her menial tasks. She was an Infermier, meaning the lowest of the staff: an assistant to the nurses and other professional staff, one of those assigned to clean up the messes. She wore a blue work smock and wooden or canvas shoes. She didn't think I noticed as she swatted the kids with a broom when they baited her.

To my surprise, she requested an interview. I'll never forget this experience, and she hasn't either. Along with five other key women from the staff, she was the first to come in and sit across from us alone. There were three of us and an interpreter. She sat with dignity, upright in her chair. Her bearing was one of humility, intimidation, and confidence all at the same time. She was dressed in her best skirt, dress shoes, and a chapeau. Her hands were folded in her lap, holding a small purse.

I asked, "Why would you like to stay and work here?"

Through the interpreter, she spoke confidently in a soft voice, never searching for words. "We have heard rumors about what you are going to do here. We understand there will be better conditions here for the children, that there will be better food, and the living conditions will be improved."

"That's true, but why do you want to be here?"

In the same gentle voice, she said: "I want to try to explain something to you. We love these children! Some of us have known them since they were babies. Try to understand what it is like to be the only person here at night, alone with fifty-two children. There is no heat and very little food. They are dirty and hungry. While you are upstairs, the children downstairs— knowing you are alone—will make a big noise. When you run downstairs to quiet them, the children upstairs will begin to make a noise. You have been here all day and you are tired. You will do things you regret. But how many of us have lived lives with circumstances we begged God for the chance to relive? If this is to be a house of new life with enough resources and training to do our work and care for these children the way they should be cared for, I want to be here."

"You're in!" we said. Some of the other members of the staff, after waiting their turn to speak with us, came with her. They became the core of a new group of caregivers.

It was the love and the courage she displayed that opened the hearts of her colleagues and enabled them to step forward and speak up. She brought with her a willingness to trust us. I'll never forget it.

Veronica Zaharia—this lovely woman worked past her mandatory retirement age until 2020, when she had to stay at home to care for her husband. She supervised the house. She was there to oversee the other women on the staff. She never stopped learning and kept impeccable records of the kids' medications as well as other medical records. She knew their clothing sizes, favorite foods, and brought them each the treats they liked. Even now she drops in for visits to see her colleagues and to cut the kids' hair. She knows each child's birthday. Along with the other women of the staff who are still with these kids today, I couldn't love and respect anyone outside my family more than I do the woman we call Vero.

There is another woman who was a colleague of Vero's from 1992. She'd be embarrassed if I used her name. She is generally of a stoic nature with an implacable expression. When I recently interviewed the staff one-on-one, she said to me, "Don't tell anyone. My face does not reflect what I feel in my heart for these children." She is still there too.

The core of a staff had emerged, but there was a home that needed to be built. The staff was critically important, but their workplace was unlivable … and winter was coming.

CHAPTER 21

Needing an Advocate

*I will ask the Father, and He will give you another Helper, so
that He may be with you forever.*

—John 14:16

With winter only eight months away, Adi and I had thirty-five
children awaiting our care with no place for them to live. From
when I'd first met them, they'd now lived beyond infancy and
toddlerhood. That meant all the cribs they'd been confined to in
large wards, even at ages five and six, needed to be discarded and
replaced by smaller rooms with bunkbeds. We needed people in
place with the skill sets required to work cohesively with special
needs children who had never known anything but isolated
confinement. In short, PC#3 as we'd known it needed to
disappear.

Adi and I set our time constraints to have the transformation
completed by November 1. The planning and setting of goals
were simple; the tasks and related time needed for accomplishing
all of what we needed to have in place weren't. A lot of tasks had
to be completed quickly and thoroughly in a setting with agencies

not known for cooperating efficiently. We needed someone to go before us and for Him to bring us advocates.

As I've mentioned, we already had our priorities for the renovations in mind. We needed an architect to give us a plan with nine family suites, allowing for four children per suite. Next, a completed set of working drawings to estimate the costs, followed by a budget approved by the US embassy facilities manager to match our grant, and a Romanian contractor able to finish the build-out quickly without too many hold-ups from unmotivated subcontractors.

Once the building neared completion, we needed to smoothly transition the installation of eighteen new imported bunk beds, new kitchen equipment, and a kitchen fully stocked with fresh and frozen foods. We needed simple hygiene products for first aid, medicines, towels, soaps, and toothbrushes. And toys. Last but not least, in order to legally cover our activities and money management processes, we needed two validly constituted not-for-profit corporations, one approved by a Romanian court and the other approved by the IRS.

Despite all this, I never felt a sense of being out of sync with the plan I was given or with my partner. Our willingness to serve each other allowed us to bring to the table what the other couldn't, and our ethnocentricities blended easily due to our shared faith. He'd registered his own tax-free foundation, and we copied the steps he'd taken to legalize Chi Rho in Romania. Forming the Romanian entity was a relatively easy thing to do. In Romania, a court has to rule on the legality of the corporation's function and approve its paperwork. A notary then reviews and approves the corporation's documentation, records it, and the applicant's identity becomes a matter of public record.

Chi Rho also needed to exist in the US, and I came back home naively expecting the process to be as easy as it had been in Romania. In fact, it did turn out to be easy, but only because the Hand on the open door provided us with four more advocates.

I was given the name of an attorney who could help me with obtaining an application from the IRS for tax-exempt status. It was said he was an advocate of more than the law. I called him, and he agreed to see me. (Our Navy connection continued here—this man is a graduate of the US Naval Academy and retired as a captain after serving as a SEAL.)

I explained to our newest advocate that I needed a foundation here in the US to collect donations to fund a hospital facility in Romania to care for special needs kids. He heard the naivete in my request. He cautiously replied that getting tax-exempt status from the IRS took time and that they could make the applicant's approval process difficult if they chose to. He wasn't perfunctory; he allowed me to explain why I didn't have much time. I described PC#3 and that its residents were sick and that the hospital had begun withholding resources for their care to stretch its own budget.

He directed his secretary to forward me the application's paperwork. When it came, my heart sank. Its contents were as indiscernible to me as hieroglyphics. I couldn't get through this morass of administrivia correctly. I needed a CFO, someone to shape the origins of Chi Rho and complete the IRS application, and I needed one fast. Who should I ask? Where would I find someone capable of giving me this much of their time? In my prayers I began to ask the Spirit to give me that person.

On Sundays I usually went to hear a friend teach a class. Listening to him was refreshing because his lessons were from personal experience, full of Biblical content, and the question-

and-answer sessions lively and thought provoking. As I sat listening to him, the Spirit said, *Ask your friend Ken.* I laughed. "He'll say no! He's been talking for weeks in his lessons about living intentionally, not extemporaneously. He's stopped volunteering and has strict boundaries for taking on anything new. He'll say no! And I barely know him."

Ask Ken.

After the class I approached him with, "Ken, I'm starting a nonprofit to fund the support for some sick HIV-positive kids in Romania. I need a CFO, and I need him to fill out the IRS application forms right away. I need your help."

He said, "Yes, I'll do it. Why don't you come by my office this week and show me what you need?"

Just like that, he said yes. I only knew Ken from attending his classes on Sundays. Beyond the context of seeing my face in his classroom, he didn't know me. That same week we met in his office, and with a thud I dropped the stack of forms on his desk and explained the urgency. I explained our attorney's admonition surrounding the approval process, and Ken said, "That's okay, I can do this. Do you play golf?"

Ken's an unusual guy. That week he'd been listening to the Spirit because he'd been complaining out loud to his wife that he had no friends to play golf with. Ken's always said his wife had the biggest crap detector he'd ever seen: "And I grew up in Brooklyn."

When she heard his lament about being lonely, she got right on him with: "Well, why would you? You never ask anybody to go with you to play, and you never do anything with anybody else. You used to but not anymore."

Ken decided that relief from his self-imposed solitude lay in living the discipline of the Beatitudes, one of which is mercy.

Mercy, he said, is simply saying yes to a need when it is within your ability to be merciful. So, Ken had resolved that for one week he would exercise the qualities of mercy and say yes to anyone who asked him for help. And, as directed by the Spirit, I happened to be one of those people. In his office, he asked me if I played golf. I did. Before we each moved to different states we played golf almost weekly and we remain spiritual friends. In less than a week he sent the completed IRS application back to our attorney, who carried the matter forward.

Some nonprofit applications can languish in the IRS offices for months, even years. Our advocate in his wisdom shared our application with a person he knew there. He said she was older, Jewish, and an attorney herself. He told me later that she had pulled the file from the stack on her desk and said, "This is the first legitimate request I've had in months. I'll get it through." When we did obtain a conditional IRS ruling in April 1998, it had only been in process for a few short weeks.

Now we had the kids, authority to manage them, and legal status in Romania and the United States. We only had one more major obstacle remaining.

On June 1, 1998, when our lease began, we had to be ready to start construction to make our November deadline. Adi and I had hoped we could manage working around the kids being in the building, but that was wishful thinking—but then so was uprooting and resettling thirty-five little children and their caregivers. All this seemed like an impossible task to manage. Where could we put them, who would take them, and for how long? What would it cost? We needed another advocate.

CHAPTER 22

The Camp

You do not have because you do not ask ... God is opposed to the proud but gives grace to the humble.

—James 4:2, 6

My brother Adi had many earthly and spiritual gifts. One of them was his skill at networking. He was good at it because he loved people. When I would judge someone, he would say to me "Hud, they're not just a person, it's a Soul." For such a pragmatic man, the grace of *his* soul was unmistakable. The people he met could feel it and they would give back when he asked for help.

Whether it was his family, the church of his own community, the church worldwide, friends old and new, or old contacts who were the remnants from his career, he was able to draw upon relationships with hundreds of people for many varied and useful purposes. After university he became a general contractor and project manager for the Romanian Agricultural Department. His work took him to most of the Romanian cities and Judets (counties) with agricultural production. He knew union leaders, city officials, and political figures from all around the country. It was why he was able to say from firsthand experience why "it takes a lot of time to live in Romania" *if you follow the rules.* It was because of his work-related connections that we found a safe, temporary domicile for the kids to stay while PC#3 was being rebuilt.

Mamaia ("Mamaya") is the name of a Black Sea beach resort in Constanta. Its miles of shoreline are lined with beachside hotels and resorts. It's well known in Europe as a summer destination. In the summer, Constanta's population swells from 300,000 in the non-summer months to more than a million as visitors come to stay at the beaches for their holiday. It makes life in the city (as you might imagine) a little crazy. But farther up the coast, a few miles from Mamaia, a labor union owned a tranquil rest-and-recreation camp, set apart for its more elite members and their families to get away from the summer heat. It had dormitories and a kitchen, playgrounds, sport courts, and access to the beach. Adi called me to say our kids and the mamas could go there to live while PC#3 was being rebuilt, beginning in July until the end of October 1998. The cost was $10,000. We jumped at it.

I went to see the camp soon after our kids and the staff moved in. As a venue for little kids to live and play, this place wasn't limited like PC#3 was. The foods available for them came in abundance, and for the first time in their lives, there was plenty to eat. I once watched at breakfast while one of our little girls, Petra, consumed eight small mixing bowls of bread and milk, one right after the other without stopping.

Petra has never been able to speak a word, but she has always been able to get what she wants. The nonverbal communication skills that the staff and the special needs kids have with each other are more than intuition. Not a word from the kids, just sounds and expressions with gestures, and their mamas know where the "conversation" is going. It is all love between them. That day at the camp, Vero and Petra's mama tried to assure Petra, reading her inquisitive expressions, that there would be more bread when she needed it. The kids who do speak asked me, "How long will this new program last?" meaning the camp and the food. "There have been other programs before, and will you be leaving us too?"

I asked the mamas if I might stay some nights with them out at the camp. Cynthia and I had our own rented flat to stay in when we came to visit. It was comfortable, and it was our "place" while we were there, but I wanted to be able to tell people at home what our staff and the kids were experiencing living at the camp. I pushed a bed into a closet and spent two nights.

The first night I awakened to the sound of Vasilica wailing. She is one of our most profoundly affected special needs kids. It was common for her and some of the others to do this; it was a horrifying thing to listen to. It was a primordial and visceral sound, and she would go on like this for hours. I lay there and listened for more than an hour when her mamas knocked on my closet door asking for help. I lay down beside Vasilica and wrapped her in my arms like a blanket. I whispered and prayed into her ear for more than an hour while I rocked her, and eventually she went to sleep. She did it again the next night, so I repeated my prayers and rocked her again, and this time she went to sleep sooner. She stopped the practice the next night and remained silent at night but for a few more incidents in later years.

In my prayers for Vasilica, I invoked the Spirit in Christ's name to fill her heart with His presence and push out the fear of evil she'd lived with as a toddler. I whispered it in her ear over and over. This was the opportunity I longed for: to be a witness to the children that their scars and doubts could be healed and replaced with God's love for them. Those memories of neglect and abuse are not forgotten, but hope can be restored when someone they learn to trust receives them in love when they cry out.

In the morning after my second night at the camp, some of my friends among the mamas—the ones I had known from the early years of visiting PC#3—came to me with smiles and said, "We know why you're here. You're spying on us." It's quintessentially Romanian to be both conspiratorial and direct about it. I told them: "No, I'm not spying on you. I want to know what this place is like for you and the kids to live in and how you're reacting to the freedom from the old regime. How can I tell the people at home what it's really like for you here?" I don't know how many of them believed me; it doesn't matter. I wanted to live like they did, in a Romanian flat or in the camp, not in a hotel like a visitor.

Truly the call on my heart to be at the camp (or for that matter in Constanta) wasn't only born out of curiosity for the place. My curiosity was driven by an interest in the staff and the kids' everyday circumstances. What indignities did they suffer and from whom or what? What were their joys? What needs did they have that they wouldn't or couldn't disclose to me? We Chi Rho Americans truly do care for them. I can't explain why it was these few rather than so many others, except that God gave them to me to be held up for people to see.

People still ask me, "Why did you go there?" Those who know the Father can understand my simple answer: I was told to go there to see what He wanted me to see. It was a call on my heart. So I wanted to know them, and I wanted them to know me. I believe by my faith in Christ that I am His body by His grace and mercy. If they knew me, then they would know Jesus and that

He loves them. It's a simple thing to lay claim to and draw power from when we accept fully Jesus's resurrection and redemptive love. For the privilege of seeing God working through me for many years, for them to come to know after many years that they're loved, and to see these least of the least and their mamas able to trust and return love ... there are no adequate words to describe what I feel in abundance!

After two nights at the camp, Adi drove out to pick me up, but before going back to my flat, he invited me to meet the director of the camp. This was the man with whom Adi had made the arrangements for the kids to have a place to live. The director wanted to speak with me because he was curious about the American man in his camp.

"Adi, I just want to go home," I said. "I'm tired, I don't want to do more socializing!" But Adi insisted I meet this man.

The camp director's office was in a freestanding building set aside from the dormitories and kitchen and dining commons. The secretary's outer office actually had a secretary in it—a blond, full-figured woman in a white dress who offered us coffee, tea, or something stronger. We waited the prescribed five minutes before being allowed into the man's private inner office. We were greeted by an imposing figure. The man was large—standing six-five with jet-black hair, a black suit and black tie, black eyeglasses, and a perfectly pressed white shirt. But contrary to his imposing size and title, he had an open smile and affable manner as he reached out his hand to shake mine. On the credenza behind him was a Glock automatic pistol, bottles of vodka, mineral water, and Romanian plum brandies. *Perfect!* I thought. *This completes the picture of the unexpected!*

That's how I met Dan, and we have become very good friends. Dan is genuinely well-meaning. He's honest, straightforward, and asks transparent questions—and as Adi would describe him to me later, "He's not a shark, Hud." Adi knew Dan's father very well from their shared experiences doing work projects during the Ceauşescu regime. Dan's father headed a very powerful Communist party labor union. Adi headed the agricultural department's construction division, and together they were able to pull a lot of strings. Adi knew of Dan and his appointed position as director of the camp, and Dan knew of Adi through the relationship with his father.

Reports of an American man working in Romania with orphaned children had piqued Dan's curiosity. His English is excellent, and after a few pleasantries he began our conversation with, "Why do you do this? It's customary for us to see women who are expatriates working here for relief organizations. Adi says you're a businessman."

Like most Romanians, Dan is of the Orthodox Church. He and my other closest friends of the Orthodox faith had been told as children by their mothers or grandmothers that if they were kind to others, they would be blessed in return. Dan described his wife as a devout woman who cared for others and prayed every day. Dan's a very caring man. He loves his wife and son, his dogs, and he openly says so. After being elected to Parliament and serving several years, he eventually retired from politics and went into teaching as a professor in the local university.

All this to say, he, too, had feelings for the needs he saw around him, but he could not allow himself to act on them. In Dan's world, such expressions of sensitivity would be seen as professional weakness, and he would be taken advantage of. You never drop your guard there. It risks appearing vulnerable. The people most willing to act and risk are the women because in a patriarchal society like Romania's, women have less to lose. Dan wanted to know why an American real estate developer would be in Romania doing what I was doing if he didn't have a God to follow and a strong belief in that God. He wanted to know which faith I followed.

In fact, my first impression of Romania in the early years after the revolution was like my first meetings with most Romanians in general, and Dan in particular. Except for the older ladies in church, the people initially seem hard, curious, businesslike, even hostile at times. When I asked people for help or for a favor, they usually wanted to understand my intent: why would I have come so far to help such insignificant people? Then, after offering expressions of appreciation for my kindness toward the children, they responded with acts of kindness to me and ultimately to the children. Just like Dan did.

But that's where the acts of kindness would usually stop. They do not initiate acts of personal self-sacrifice there except for family. Acts of community service would be an infringement on the franchise of the government's programs of social assistance or municipal responsibility and lead a caring soul to a dead end, or worse it might even invite retribution from the government. The evangelical churches there reach out more than the Orthodox Church does for the opportunity to evangelize, but as individuals, the Orthodox friends I have made were willing to help because they perceived the need and gave what they could generously.

This became even more evident shortly after the kids had moved back into the House of New Life, after I had returned home. I phoned Adi to say it had been several weeks since we'd moved into CVN and I hadn't seen a bill from the camp yet. He said the $10,000 obligation to stay there for three months had been forgiven.

The life the kids and staff experienced in the camp was a gentle precursor of their new life to come. Chi Rho budgeted for their needs now. Their menu changed; for the first time it became varied and nourishing, and there was enough for them take in as much or as little as they wished. Their clothing became gender-specific and individually fitted. Laundry was picked up and cleaned by their mamas, who now had access to washing machines. And for the first time ever, they could swing on swing sets and play on the slides. They could walk to the beach and buy treats in the magazine stands that catered to tourists, or their mamas would bring gifts and homemade treats.

We had always wanted to know who they were. Cynthia and I arranged with CVN's assistant director to interview each child. We sat on the steps and talked to all of them, each child one at a time. For those who could talk, we asked them: "What's your name? What's your favorite color? What's your favorite food? What do you want to be when you grow up? How old are you?"

One of the few answers I remember was Bumba saying, "I am grown up!" What he was really saying was, "I'm still alive!" He went on to say he wanted to be a pilot.

But those beautiful moments were still to come. While the children were still at the camp, our tranquility was rudely broken when one afternoon we found the mamas crying. The hospital staff had come out to the camp in the vans to pick up the kids for testing without warning. They simply walked in, grabbed the ones they wanted by the arm while the kids shrieked in terror and the mamas protested, and tossed them into the vans. The kids knew what was coming in the form of large adult-sized needles for withdrawing blood samples to support the doctor's experiments. There were no experiments of a meaningful nature at that time to warrant such data gathering; antiretrovirals (ARVs) weren't being distributed yet. The doctor simply viewed the kids as her property and was reasserting her authority.

I'm not exaggerating. When the children were returned that afternoon, there were tears and hugs and laughter throughout the entire new Chi Rho family, but their hopes for peace had been trampled on as the perpetrator of the incident had known they would be. It had been a power play. The new life that we had promised was one the kids and their mamas believed in, and clearly confrontation was going to be required to protect it. We asked the hospital to let us know when they needed to see the kids and respect our schedule of daily activities so we could prepare the kids and make room for their mamas to go with them to the hospital for their tests, as any normal mother and her child would.

When the doctor ignored us and grabbed the kids again after they had moved back into their new home at Casa Viata Noua, I confronted the nurse we were required by our agreement with the hospital to keep as a supervising presence. This nurse was one of the doctor's enforcers and the former director of PC#3, and I told her point-blank: "If you don't agree to these conditions, I'll call the police and tell them you're abducting our children against our wishes. I'll lock the front door until the police come to provide us with protection. Tell the doctor she has no authority here unless she chooses to cooperate." I'd hoped it wouldn't come to that, but delicious irony—the tables had turned.

My objection was sustained, and our staff and the new director henceforth insisted our sovereignty as a family be respected. This was new life indeed in Romania.

One of my favorite memories of that time and that new life came during a summer afternoon in 1998, just before I left for home. We had one final thing to do before Adi took me to the airport. We drove out to see the work going on in PC#3. We stood in front of the building for a few minutes and stared at what we were seeing. PC#3 was disappearing. During our careers we had both seen construction sites many times. But the impact of this construction activity caused us to stand immobile and simply stare at the building.

Then without speaking, we unconsciously reached for each other and linked arms like two old men would do to support themselves, and we walked together through the front door. We went from room to room holding on to each other, still not saying a word. Workmen glanced up at us, shrugged at the sight, said nothing, and went on about their work.

When we returned to his car, we sat staring out the front window for a few moments, still not saying anything, until I finally said, "Adi, you and I have seen the sun, moon, and stars, and our own children being born right in front of us. That ought to be miracle enough in a lifetime. But when we walk through a building under construction like we've both seen a hundred times, we're speechless. How do you explain that?"

"Hud, when you think of what God had to do to bring this about, it is a miracle. He had to take down the Iron Curtain, bring down a government, and remove Ceaușescu, or you wouldn't have been able to get here. We both had to become Christians, and we had to meet. He arranged for the government to give us this place. And He did all of that to save some children nobody wanted. All these things are a miracle, and that's why we're speechless."

Which was an absolute truth—and leads me to my best recollection. From June until November 1998, PC#3 was rebuilt. We took down the government sign over the doorway, *Post Cura #3*, and replaced it with a new sign and a new name that reads, *Casa Viata Noua*, or *House of New Life*. Underneath the name is a passage from Mark 10:14: "Allow the children to come to Me; do not forbid them, for the kingdom of God belongs to such as these."

God had directed us to us a filthy, rundown "medical prison" with sick and dying special needs children. Watching Him transform it grew my faith for the storm yet to come.

CHAPTER 23

Doubts and Patience

"If you would direct your heart rightly
And spread out your hands to Him,
If wrongdoing is in your hand, put it far away ...
And you would be firmly established and not fear."

—Job 11:13-15

Winters in Constanta can be very cold. Its place on the globe is
farther north than the latitude of Chicago, and like the Windy
City, it's situated next to a large body of water. The prevailing
winds that bring Siberian temperatures from the steppe and
across the Black Sea have nothing to interrupt their travel. There
are times the Black Sea freezes. People attempting travel between
Bucharest and Constanta during the severe winters put their lives
at risk, sliding off the icy roads or becoming isolated in heavy
snowdrifts and freezing to death before they can be rescued. For
the impatient or unprepared traveler, Romanian winters are
inhospitable and unsympathetic.

My time for this 1999 visit was over, and I wanted to go home.
I was wrung out. The Romanian hospital and social services had

beaten me down, but getting home wasn't a foregone conclusion. That year, winter was very cold with more than the usual amount of snow. The road from Constanta to Bucharest was closed to all car and truck traffic, allowing only for train travel between the cities. Doubts about getting home at all had set into my heart.

Notwithstanding the weather, many other things would have to go right in order for me to get home. To this day, after more than sixty round trips—that's 778,800 miles or thirty-one times around the Earth—I never take getting home for granted. The odds are against it. When I get out of bed in Constanta and take my first step of the morning to begin the journey, my prayer is, "If it is in your will, Father, I would like to go home now." And every time I arrive home safely, I thank God for directing my steps.

The naivete of some has led me to hear things like, "If you're in God's will, doubts will never enter in." When I ponder those ideas, I keep this thought to myself: *I wonder whose will you're in?* I know of no honest relationship that is void of doubt from time to time. If God is more than an idea, you'll be hearing from Him—and if you're following Him, doubt is a normal emotion to experience as a consequence of this or any other mission.

By the end of 1999, I had a lot of new reasons to doubt His purposes, and travel was the least of them. Now that the kids were in their new home and the lid of abuse had been lifted, the spectrum of needs they exhibited spewed out in a torrent of vile expressions and rebellious behaviors. After the State's abuse—attempting to institutionally euthanize them—our kids were now receiving individual recognition and nurturing love from their caregivers. However, in their new living circumstances—coming as suddenly as they did—the contrast of the present with their past was too much for them. They'd never learned how to trust another human. They had doubts, too, and expressed them in the only way they knew how.

To be absolutely clear, the children's circumstances were much better than they had been. We had what we wanted: we were in the newly remodeled House of New Life and they couldn't lock us out. The kids' day-to-day routines were ours to manage. They were no longer the doctor's and the hospital administration's pediatric lab rats for HIV research. Still, as I wrote out my trip report, the range of needs was growing and the need to find resources to meet them was adding to the complexity of our program.

Each child bore the psychological scars of abuse and abandonment. Out of the original cohort of thirty-six kids that we at Chi Rho began with that first day on June 1, 1998, thirty-two kids remained in our care, and all but two of them were HIV-positive. I have reported different numbers of kids in PC#3 when I first visited and later under Chi Rho's care in 1998, because until June 1998, they were moved around from place to place and I had no authority to ask why they were changed out. When I first visited in 1992, I was told fifty-six kids lived in PC#3, but later I was told that number was fifty-two. Nobody could reconcile the difference in those two numbers. On June 1, 1998, we began with thirty-six because, although Ribana had died, she was for now ours to care for, even in death. Of the remaining thirty-five, two were adopted, and Adi Secure succumbed to the virus, which left us with thirty-two. From then on, some returned to their families or were placed in foster care, and we had children die in both settings. Some remain in foster care and are doing well. Three more were given to us by the hospital staff with the hope that they would receive a chance at life under our care. Some of the higher-functioning kids went on to live independent lives, some successfully, others not. As of this writing one young lady is hospitalized for severe schizophrenia, and we support her expenses, which leaves just nine who will require lifelong care.

The kids' CD4 counts and viral loads accounted for their inability to recover easily from normal childhood diseases, which were made even more contagious by their close surroundings and lack of sepsis prevention in the old PC#3. (A normal CD4 count means that your immune system is not yet significantly affected by HIV. Viral load refers to the amount of virus in an infected person's blood. So if the two numbers are expressed as a ratio in a patient, a high viral load and a low CD4 count means the life expectancy of the patient is lower.) Solutions to these dilemmas were made more complex by the workplace habits of the Romanian culture. The vertical top-down method of instruction and management put all the responsibility for problem-solving on the person at the top. If our staff wasn't prepared to learn as much as they could and how to delegate responsibility to each other, then we were just another funding organization. I wanted us to be engaged with each other and the kids like any large healthy family.

The kids bore complex medical and profound psychological wounds, but by far the worst were the psychological wounds. Those will never be healed. Our particular kids were the detritus of the orphanage system of warehousing unwanted children. They were the product of the doctor's method of systematic selection of her HIV cases. Ours were the survivors, the kids with emotional resolve; they were the ones who had lived. The more "normal" and beautiful kids had been moved out. Those with the most acute special needs or rebellious natures had been sent to us. Some suffered from fetal drug and alcohol syndrome; all of them had experienced nutritional, emotional, physical, and sometimes sexual abuse while in the care of the pediatric infectious disease hospital. We thought the Romanian hospitals, doctors, and dentists would help us with the kids' medical needs, but help with the emotional needs would have to come from us and our staff.

As it turned out, neither was available to the degree we needed. I thought we'd be applauded for what we'd done. Instead, I was openly questioned by hospital officials and even friends from the Romanian church about my motives. "They are better off dying," they said. "Who will care for them when you leave like all the others have and they are let out on society? Why are you interrupting a normal process of elimination? We want this part of our history to be left behind us and disappear and the kids along with it." Some believe to this day that we were only there to sell their body parts when they died.

Talk about having doubts. What had I gotten myself into? Maybe the Romanians were right. I'd uncovered the consequences of a generation of iniquity. There was no turning back now, and I'd even begged God to let me do this. If they did live, there would be no fairy tale ending for these kids, but the commitment to shepherding them stretched out for as long as they lived. Who would take responsibility for them from six thousand miles away for the rest of their lives? Who would pay for it? How much would it cost? Maybe it was best to look away, affect a remorseful stance and say, "I'm sorry, I did my best; what can I do?"

I wanted to go home, find peace, and get away from the murky confusion that surrounded me and left me feeling hypoxic. At that moment, I seriously doubted if I could even get home. Furthermore, to find the comforts of home I longed for I had to abandon the place where God had called me to be in His will. At home my heart would be in two places, leaving it in a state of uncertainty for several months. I would be abandoning the friends and the children I loved and had pledged to support to the chaos and uncertainty of a completely countercultural paradigm. All of what I had seen Him accomplish and everything I wanted to see happen in the future would fall back into confusion and be reversed.

Still, I felt I had abandoned my family at home, being gone for two weeks at a time, once for an entire month. Was I indulging a whim by going to Romania to see some helpless kids? To say that I had doubts was an understatement.

Still, there was no doubt that Casa Viata Noua was a totally new normal. The staff and the kids were being deinstitutionalized, untrained, hopefully to learn their value as individuals in God's sight. We had divided the kids into eight "families." By compartmentalizing the staff and kids into surrogate family units, we could observe the interaction of the mamas, the interaction of the kids with their new mamas, and the interaction of the kids among each other. The smaller units made it easier to observe and evaluate them than when they were in large unsupervised groups or sequestered in isolated rooms as was the case in the old PC#3.

Our expatriate director gave the families numbers. Later, our team gave them the names of objects in nature such as Iris, Rose, or Sunflower. To the team, the names of flowers seemed less institutional.

But there were still challenges ahead. The hospital didn't provide dental care for their unwanted patients, and the medical care wasn't normal pediatric maintenance. Our agreement with the hospital required us to hire a nurse from the doctor's foundation and give her an office in the house to work out of. She was nothing more than the doctor's eyes and ears to watch us. It was a terrible job; she had nothing to do but sit in the small office near the kitchen and smoke.

In the 1990s, pharmaceutical companies and doctors doing research in infectious disease looked into Romania and saw the cohort of HIV patients. They wanted access to the kids for experiments and testing and were willing to support the cost. I was beginning to understand the magnitude of the kids' special needs when I heard the incredible news from our staff that antiretroviral drugs (ARVs) were being administered through the Constanta Infectious Disease Hospital. I heard some kids in the system were getting these drugs, but obviously ours were not yet. At first, I pressed gently with the question, "Why not?" The first answer that came back was that because of the expense there were not enough of the drugs to go around. When I asked who was providing the cost of the drugs, at first no one knew who was supporting the program. Pressing harder on our staff that had hospital relationships, I was told that it was because our kids were "encephalopat," or special needs—the drugs were not to be made available to kids who were "idiots."

These were the two components to be measured on an internal graph in my heart. As the vertical line on the doubts component increased, the pressure I felt suppressing indignation also increased. How long could I stand to wait for someone other than myself to initiate on behalf of the children's needs? Did anyone even see the needs? The patience component was on a flat horizontal plane, and it stretched out indefinitely. After a year and a half of being in place, I came to learn that the hospital viewed us as nothing more than a dormitory for them. Our kids were lab rats for the doctor's specious experiments. We were paying for their upkeep and saving the hospital money. To change the kids' medical regime by providing ARVs would mean altering her experimental treatments, thus rendering the data coming out of them invalid. We would have to tell her to stop her experimental treatments and provide ARVs ourselves. She would lose her support and her gatekeeper status due to the efforts of an outsider who wasn't paying her. She would not give that up willingly. And for what, lives considered to be throwaways?

On a freezing cold winter day when I heard definitively that the ARVs weren't to be made available, it struck me. If they wouldn't give me ARVs for my kids, I would provide them. I'd force the doctor to compete with me. I walked out of the house and stood in the street so the staff wouldn't hear me yelling. The ice in the street was clear blue; it was windy and snowing lightly. I looked up and yelled, "Are You telling me I have to do a clinic? Where am I going to find a clinic?"

My eyes fell on the building on the corner of Strada Ion Ionescu de la Brad and Strada Medeea. It was a bombed-out wreck of a broken-down building with tilted walls, broken glass, and barbed wire. The interiors were a haven for strays and the homeless. For several years we had walked by it, trying to ignore it for the offense it was to our senses. I said to Him, "You have got to be kidding!"

He was not kidding. After forcing my way through a rusted door, I knelt down on the floor of the building amid broken glass and dog feces and offered my gratitude in a prayer: "If it be in Your will Father, let me do this."

I would need a doctor, money for the ARVs—which were very expensive then—and money to buy a building and remodel it into a modern medical facility. I thought He could do it; I had no doubt

He could if that's what He wanted. I received admonitions from the Spirit: *Don't do this out of anger or it will not end well.*

My goals for moving into the House of New Life had been simple: I wanted each child to know I loved them. I wanted to restore their hope. I wanted them to live with dignity and to make their own choices. But in removing the abuse and neglect that had kept them cowed and subservient, I had released their demons—and not just at our house. The needs that emerged out of the shadows of the Romanian orphanages will never be overcome. We were trying to encourage our kids to live, but if they did, there would be consequences. In fact, as I have written this, the needs have multiplied because most of them from our house have survived—something we didn't think would happen. Those few high-functioning kids grew up to have children of their own, and some of those children have also been abandoned. Some of our kids (all of whom are HIV-positive) have been trafficked in other countries, too much in need to say no to those who've exploited them again.

In 1999, I hadn't seen this future yet because I could not have thought that far ahead without having had serious doubts. I naturally defaulted to the thought that the kids would probably die because the "consequences" of their living that I spoke of earlier were too vast and unimaginable. In the meantime, they were my children to be cared for as if they were my own. The "system," on the other hand, could see the downside if the kids lived, and it had turned away from the psychological, psychiatric, medical, and dental needs of the kids. To the system, their mistakes should die with the kids. To expect that the doctor, even as a pediatrician and the system's gatekeeper, would look into the medical care of the ones the system had discarded was naïve on my part.

Yet along with the doubts and misgivings came blessings.

One of my favorite things to do was to sit in the kitchen in a wooden chair leaning up against a wall while the mamas prepared the lunches. They would laugh and kid me for such a simple pleasure and for being a man in the kitchen. I would stare out at the sky through the windows set high up on the wall and listen. I listened to the cooks laughing at each other and shooing kids out of the kitchen after giving one of them a cookie. I listened to life in the house going on around me and compared it to the morbid sound of silence and sadness that had been life in PC#3. I listened to the Spirit and offered Him thanks.

Just before both of us left for home, I had a rapid-paced conversation with the first director. Her two-year tenure was about to be over, and I had managed to find an hour alone with her to hear what she had observed from the kids' behaviors and the mamas' reactions to them. What we had hoped to learn about the children was why we had made the enormous effort to come and stay. I didn't know why she'd been reluctant in giving me detailed explanations of the kids' former circumstances and a description of their emerging personalities. Operational matters seemed to be easier for her to discuss, but the kids' needs drove the planning necessary to manage the operational matters. They were our children; we wanted to know what special treatment they needed for us to succeed in building new lives for them and helping them to find hope and be able to return the love they were receiving.

I took voluminous notes during our conversation, many of which you can read in the Appendix to this book. It's my hope that you'll explore these notes with a tender heart because their conditions *are* difficult to read through. I considered each child to be my own and so I poured over these notes to get them right. I'm proud of them!

On that 1999 flight home, somewhere between Iceland and Greenland, I was sitting alone looking out my window. I was going home to see Cynthia after several weeks of being apart. It was night; I was the only one on the plane who was awake. I looked out across the wing at the Swiss cross painted on the port winglet of the DC-10 and tried to imagine what the outside temperature would feel like. It was winter at 35,000 feet over the North Atlantic. It must be so cold that the impact of the temperature would feel like icy needles! I said to the Father, "You're out there, too, in that terrible extreme. What a wonderful God you are, letting me work for You, and now You're sending me home. Thank You." Then His hands reached through the window and held my face. His hands were warm. *You are my son. You have done what I asked you to do. Now, watch this.*

Through the cabin window, a small green dot appeared to the right of my peripheral vision, like a single dot on a dot matrix computer screen. It forced me to look again to see if my senses hadn't betrayed me, and it was there again, but it began to grow. Larger and larger, the window began to be filled with a glowing green and blue curtain of pulsating colors. They danced and swirled across the entire spectrum of the window! I wanted to shout, to wake up the plane, but that would only disturb them. I got up and walked to the galley and told the Swiss Air cabin attendant, "Look! Look out there." She was startled at the lights that glowed in the frigid night.

"I've been traveling these routes for twenty years," she said. "I've never seen the Northern Lights."

CHAPTER 24

Foster Care

"Listen to this! Laments coming out of Ramah,
wild and bitter weeping.
It's Rachel weeping for her children,
Rachel refusing all solace.
Her children are gone,
gone—long gone into exile."
But God says, "Stop your incessant weeping,
hold back your tears.
Collect wages from your grief work." God's Decree.
"They'll be coming back home!
There's hope for your children." God's Decree.

—Jeremiah 31:15-16 The Message

By the spring of 2000, references to PC#3 as a place name had faded away. Place names and identities seem to morph on their own. In our case, the House of New Life took too long for us to say, so it became CVN, the acronym for Casa Viata Noua. The Romanians referred to CVN as Chi Rho. But even though PC#3 had disappeared, for those who had lived or worked there, the scars of that former life were indelible. And not just for the kids. In the year 2000, many other people—like Marolen—had come from around the world, trying to help the hundreds of other kids in need scattered across Romania.

On this particular day, we learned that one of those helpers had settled in the offices of a US senator in Washington, D.C. Cynthia and I were at home that day when I heard her coming to find me. She usually has a question when she does that.

"Who do you know in Washington, D.C.?"

"I don't know anybody. Why?"

"There's a fax coming in just now addressed to you from a US senator and the Romanian ambassador—something about a meeting they're sponsoring with the Romanian embassy and a senate committee. They're inviting people working in Romania to come to Washington. It's going to be at the Romanian embassy in D.C. You can read it."

"How did they get our fax number?"

"I don't know. Are you going to go?"

"I guess so."

The arrival of the fax triggered other thoughts, and this one not for the first time: Is our work that unusual that they need to be able to find us? It always seems to follow that when you go somewhere unusual to do something no one else wants to do, you get noticed. The blessing of working anonymously in my profession is that it requires no self-promotion. But the irony of touching a need is that it prompts others to see the work, and that leads to them wanting to know more. Questions follow, starting with, "Why do you do this?" My answers are usually the same. I tell them God asked me to go there or I was called there, which prompts more questions. But what did a senator want to know?

At that time, Romania was being considered for membership

in the European Union and NATO. Among the conditions of acceptance into either body were two nexus issues relating to children. One condition required Romania to end the corruption associated with foreign adoptions. The other was a Children's Bill of Rights the Romanian parliament was expected to enact, which included a package of benefits that should be paid out to the survivors of the Romanian orphanages in the form of support. Romania's political leadership wanted its diplomats to manage the EU and NATO negotiations over the conditions for entry carefully because being a member nation meant gaining access to EU grants, loans to finance their foreign debt, and development funds for NATO projects. That remunerative package was far too great an incentive to lose by appearing impassive or indifferent to the concerns the EU and NATO member nations had for the way orphaned children should be treated, at least for now while the conditions for entry were being negotiated. The senator had to have miscalculated the outcome of her agenda by inviting active foreign NGOs to come to an open gathering and endorse the good intentions of the Romanian state department.

I went to the meeting at the Romanian embassy, my curiosity piqued about the senator's agenda. Maybe she'd reveal it or perhaps by meeting her and some of the other attendees, I could acquire some favors for Chi Rho. I don't remember the invitation's agenda, but I recall having no expectations of making a contribution. In my business, we would call events like these "love feasts." People meet to feel good about their shared passions and do networking. It didn't end that way, though.

The meeting began at ten in the morning in the embassy's enormous great room. Conference tables were arranged in a giant square to manage what looked like about one hundred people. It was chaired by the senator and—the Romanians' participation notwithstanding—it was clearly her affair. She opened the meeting with the usual greetings, followed by the current Romanian ambassador to the US and his replacement, followed by some NGO figures chosen by the senator's staff. The speakers began by thanking the attendees for coming and speaking of their gratitude for our work caring for the children and Romania's cooperation in helping us do our work.

Then the senator opened the discussion by asking the attendees to offer their suggestions about what further contributions the Romanians could make toward removing regulatory barriers and expediting the NGOs accomplishing their missions. Or to put it in more direct terms, "Attendees, can you give us examples of red tape to be cut to speed up the delivery of your relief efforts?" One or two of the first people to speak tried politely to discount the hypocrisy of "Romania's cooperation in helping us do our work." When the first person with the nerve to complain about the Romanian bureaucracy's road blocks, their red tape, and the mutually exclusive issue of corruption, the rest of the speakers followed suit without any hesitation, and the intensity of the discourse escalated.

People were angry. The opening statements made by the diplomats expressing their appreciation for the work of the attendees should have been left unsaid. Their platitudes were diplomatic but obviously disingenuous and only fueled the rising sarcasm of the NGOs' comments and their questions directed at the diplomats.

The issue for the NGOs wasn't the corruption, red tape or lack of cooperation from Romania associated with adoptions or a bill of rights, per se. It was the ambivalent level of sympathy and a lack of a sense of urgency from the Romanian government, at least equal to the NGOs' perception, of the terrible predicament the kids were (are) in. This message was borne out that day in the criticism given by the NGOs to the Romanian diplomats in attendance: the Romanian government does not care about the lives of their orphaned children.

It's my belief that the real cause of their anger wasn't just the corruption and red tape. It was the pain of abandoning the field and leaving behind the kids they'd come to care for because their costs were becoming unsustainable. They had painted themselves into a corner and that was the real reason that prompted my fellow NGO's angry outbursts: it was the pain in their hearts. The Romanians saw it coming, the NGOs didn't. "Let them play with some kids," I heard one man say. "We're not getting paid to care for them. NGOs will support our costs, we'll make money, everybody's happy."

The foster care program we initiated at the House of New Life wasn't about conflating anti-corruption measures, children's rights, and bureaucratic ambivalence. Chi Rho didn't need Romania's entry into the community of nations to end Romania's corruption, downsize its bureaucracies, and simplify their regulations before it cared for its kids. By the time any of those kinds of changes were made, the kids would have been dead. As it turned out, with Romania's entry into the EU and NATO, the number of the agencies and their bureaucracies grew, the regulations the EU initiated with the newly created Romanian agencies increased, and the relevance of the regulations imposed on the NGOs who remain in Romania were so ubiquitous as to be meaningless. For example, at The House of New Life we were required by our regulating agency to write our own Bill of Rights. The provisions of the document were to notify our kids at CVN of their rights and the remedies afforded them should they be mistreated. Their Bill of Rights must be posted where the kids we care for can read them. The agency that required them never came to see CVN. Had they, whoever they sent would've seen that not one of our special needs kids can read.

The town hall meeting didn't need to take place. What infuriated the NGOs wasn't our Romanian host's need or our own senator's encouraging them for more regulation of the NGO's activities. The NGOs wanted less regulation from Romania and more cooperation and financial support. The diplomats could've simply uttered "mea culpa" privately to the Senator, avoided the "town hall" meeting altogether and the acrimony could've been avoided.

One final irony. By the time I attended this meeting, I had been visiting Romania for eight years. Some very bright Romanians had been gentle but quick to remind me about the truth of American bureaucracies and our own corruption whenever I became too critical of theirs. Witness the IRS and the VA, to name only two examples.

Likewise, ethnocentricity had reared its divisive head at the meeting of NGOs in Washington. I left the embassy recalling Jesus telling Jews that the hero of one of His stories was a Samaritan, people the Jews despised. In the parable of the Good Samaritan, did the man lying by the side of the road beaten and left for dead ask to see the Samaritan's emergency health care certificate before allowing himself to be cared for? Or did the Samaritan ask to see the innkeeper's bill of rights regulations posted on his walls to prevent the abuse of wounded travelers before committing the robber's victim to the innkeeper's care? Of course, there are abusers, but privilege of authority and ethnicities aren't the point of Jesus's parable. Jesus tells the legalistic expert the parable story to explain what qualities God Himself values most. The value of mercy had been missed that morning and it left those practicing it saddened.

I hadn't anticipated what I might say that day, but I wanted Chi Rho to be noticed, and I wanted the Romanians to think someone appreciated their dilemma, if not rhetorically. I stood up to ask our group of NGOs, "What did we expect to find in our adopted country? Did we expect to find our native cultures in Romania? All of us have experienced many of the same frustrations over there. But the problem of thousands of institutionalized kids exists because of bureaucracy and corruption, and it isn't our call to end either one. Our call is to the needs of the kids." That comment was my sole contribution. My anchor against becoming disillusioned that day was Ecclesiastes 5:8: "If you see oppression of the poor and denial of justice and righteousness in the province, do not be shocked at the sight; for one official watches over another official, and there are higher officials over them."

Avoidance behavior isn't the road less traveled; it's the one most commonly taken. What all of us had been hearing in the deluge of complaints directed to the Romanian diplomats were the rationalizations of our own instincts for survival—the reasons why so many NGOs were abandoning the field out of frustration and feeling sick about leaving the kids behind.

The senator had a passion for adoption, and she wanted Romanian foreign adoptions to continue. She'd invited international adoption agencies along with the rest of us to attend the meeting to exercise our collective influence on the Romanian negotiators. That was naïve. The Romanians had openly acknowledged the corruption associated with the adoptions; they had also acknowledged that the corruption is indigenous to their government and couldn't be stopped. It wasn't logical for them to end corruption in order to gain acceptance as an EU member. After all, corruption was alive and well among the other member nations, and to expect differently from Romania was both naive and hypocritical. To gain acceptance and membership into the EU and NATO, Romania figuratively threw the babies out with the bathwater. In 2001, the Romanian parliament published a moratorium on any further foreign adoptions.

CHAPTER 25

Hope

---

*"For I know the plans that I have made for you, declares the
Lord, plans for welfare and not for calamity to give you
a future and a hope."*

—Jeremiah 29:11-14

CVN had given our kids hope. Hope came with a desire to live for
more than just the basics. They were moving up the hierarchy of
needs. They weren't experiencing life as survivors any longer; we'd
given them a life with choices, and they reached for that life. It's said
you never stop being a parent. Something we hadn't expected from
their extended lives was that our commitment as surrogate parents
was lengthening too. Imagine yourself telling your child, "I'm sorry
I didn't expect you to live this long. I don't have the personal
resources and resolve to help you manage any longer." Our
remodeled building had everything we needed for a population of
nursery school- and elementary school-aged kids but not teenagers.
Without moving a single wall, our living space was becoming
smaller as the kids got bigger physically and emotionally. Teenagers

shouldn't share the same bedrooms and bathrooms. They were going to experience puberty. Our kids, apart from the special needs aspect of their emerging natures, had no learned skills to manage these changes. They knew few inhibitions.

At CVN, life for the kids came with a different experience than the one before CVN. In the institutions they were isolated, ignored, and neglected. CVN came with love and a life to be shared with other individuals. Still, no matter how hard we tried to be families, Casa Viata Noua remained institutionalized living. They were outgrowing CVN, and as teens they would need even more careful parenting than we could provide in that kind of setting.

The sudden awareness of the need to place the kids in homes came in early 2000. There are no words to adequately express how difficult that would be. Before the 2001 foreign adoption moratorium took effect, two of our kids had been placed in foreign adoption shortly after the house opened because those two were different. Unlike some of the kids from the institutions, Nicu and Coca didn't have special needs. They had learned to project a sunny, cheerful disposition to get the attention they needed. For the rest, I would need homes with families willing to parent a difficult child. Most of our kids came with two strikes against them in Romania. Some were from Roma families, and they came with profound special needs. Their appearance alone was an obstacle. When I explained foster care or adoption and the reason behind it to the staff, they were doubtful. Speaking bluntly on the matter, one staffer said, "Nobody wants these kids." I wanted to—but didn't—respond with, "If you believe that, you're in the wrong place."

I should have waited for His insight, but my fear led to impatience. "Perhaps the adoption agency people I met in Washington can help me." After lobbying both agencies for at least six months, I don't remember which of them said, "Hud, I love what you're trying to do, but you're too small for us to devote that many resources to your cohort of kids." She was actually being kind when she said it, and her tone was sad. She could see the circumstances the kids' lives would take if Chi Rho's care collapsed. To this day, I still appreciate her clarity and honesty, even if I still don't understand what she meant by "too small."

The need to find homes for the children came with an ugly reality check for me. Failing to find a home for as long as they needed one meant I, too, would have failed them. I would have taken them to a precipice and then left them there. I'd have been better off not coming than offering them hope and then walking away. Everybody in their lives had failed them: their parents who deserted them, the system that exploited them, and their government that did both. It was this ugly truth that was at the root of the other NGOs' frustrations with the government that day in Washington. We NGOs had painted ourselves into a corner of our own making. The Romanians knew it, saw it coming, and were unprepared and unwilling to save us. Going to Romania and expecting help, NGOs became disillusioned when it didn't come and left.

My hope came from this truth: Christ left us but not Fatherless. His Spirit came, and the body of Christ emerged. He was in this work at Chi Rho, and He was in me. He would have a way for us.

Six months or more had passed waiting for an answer. No one had come to offer a plan. God speaks through the circumstances, but now I found myself yelling at Him again: "Are You telling me that we have to become our own placement agency? How do I do that?"

You won't, Hud, I will. Start by going to see Sanda Iordache.

"Sanda? She won't do that. She'll say no. We don't even have a plan."

I had met Sanda in passing at a World Vision press conference in Constanta in 1998. It was a very brief encounter. Our director knew Sanda from previous work experience at the infectious disease hospital there; she pointed Sanda out to me as she walked into the meeting precisely on time.

"There goes a good one," she said.

"Why?" I asked.

"Because she doesn't take any crap from the system."

"What does that mean?" I asked.

"She only does what she says she can do and no more. They keep trying to give her more responsibilities or to take on more kids, but she turns them down. She has an infant nursery near the sea."

On her way out after the press conference, our director introduced us. Sanda didn't stay very long, saying nothing more than polite hellos. In passing, I asked to go see what she was doing. "Sure," she said. "Come anytime."

One way to understand Sanda Iordache is as an entrepreneur in social services. She would say she does nothing, and that's partially true. Like the character Charlotte in the children's story Charlotte's Web, Sanda will describe her role as the one who sits in the upper corner of the room watching the players in the story and waits to connect them with her threads. She understands people's needs and connects them to other people with similar needs.

I returned to Romania with the intention of enlisting Sanda's help, but our in-country director was reluctant to go with me. Nonetheless, we both went to the first meeting. Our director was opposed to the idea of a Chi Rho placement program out of concern that we weren't professionals, but I wasn't sure which side of the question Sanda would come down on. I thought she'd say, "Let's start something and try it out," or "Build a construct around a professionally planned and staffed program."

Sanda was an implacable person, so I got right to the point. I explained our dilemma. Eventually the kids would outgrow CVN. I'd been unable to find a professional placement organization to help us relocate them in families. We needed an exit strategy or our kids' futures didn't look good. Would she be willing to start up and direct a program for Chi Rho that would place our kids in homes?

"How long is your commitment?"

"As long it takes."

"What are your resources?" Here I fudged a little bit, but only because I didn't know her well enough to invoke our Father's name. "They're unlimited."

"Do you have a program outline?"

"No. I was hoping you could help us with that."

Our director's comments then were, "If you're going to originate an entirely new program, it's important to start by establishing some guidelines for evaluating parents in order to meet certain standards. And caregivers can't be motivated purely by the stipend, or you'll set up some real problems for the kids. There needs to be some filters."

"No, that's not what you need. You need this." As she spoke, Sanda raised her thumb and forefinger and rubbed them together next to her nose. "You don't need elaborate filters; filters eliminate people because no one can fit into those requirements. Filters and guidelines don't find the right people; other people with the right instincts and experience do. In work like this, when you've found people willing to meet the need, then you make up the rules to support them."

Hearing her speak those words, I realized I'd experienced the same awakening when Adi leaned out to look over at me from the conference table in the basement of the Baptist church eight years earlier. "I agree with you," he'd said. "That is the basis upon which I can have a relationship." The basis of Adi's and my relationship was sharing our broken hearts. I didn't know yet how Sanda's was broken. I saw a simple heart willing to show mercy to others, and I wanted her to say, "Yes, I'll start your program."

But she didn't. Not right away. It wasn't until after my third flight over to visit her that year, when I asked her if she'd considered accepting my proposal, that she said: "Oh come on, Hud, you know I like doing the unlikely things! Sure, I'll try. We'll do the best we can." As we walked out of her nursery, she added: "But I won't lead it. I don't start programs; I take them over. I won't work for Chi Ro. I'd like to come over to CVN and see what's going on and sit in some of your meetings." That was my first glimpse into the Sanda Iordache style of management. It wasn't like anything I'd seen before in Romania, so it wasn't what my Romanian colleagues expected from her either.

A Chi Rho foster care plan had its roots in my first visit to see Sanda in her nursery in 1998. Watching her at work, there was never a question of who was in charge, but she was never issuing orders. Her staff knew what to do, and they worked together smoothly and energetically. There was never any apparent apathy, like so many of the hospital settings I had seen. From my periodic visits to her nursery, I knew she understood how to repatriate children to their families and in many cases to their unwed mothers. She was passionate about it.

The first place she looked to place the child was back with the child's mother or family. She would say, "There are no perfect families, and it's better for the child to be with their parents than in an institution." In my idealism, I believed parents who could accept abandonment weren't trustworthy with a child's life. But she knew more than I did about the outcome of abandoning a child to the system.

I learned more of who my friend was after the foster program was in place. Does that seem backward? I didn't need to know the "why" of her as a person. The urgency of the need and the absence of any other solutions to place the kids allowed for her most important qualification to be that she was willing to help. Between 1998 when CVN opened and 2000, we had visited Sanda's nursery often. In those two years, I assumed her nursery was one of the better-functioning components of the official system. As we drove the countryside outside Constanta to visit the kids in their new foster settings or had dinner in the evenings after work, there was time away from her nursery to learn more about my friend. She does not give herself quickly. The magnitude of the tragedies she's witnessed during her years working in the orphanage and social welfare system have developed her focus on what she can do, not wishful thinking.

I learned that her nursery program had been initiated by Sanda herself. Because of her reputation for integrity and efficiency over the years of her service, the right people who could support opportunities within the social welfare system trusted her and supported her budget. But her nursery was eventually shut down by new regulations requiring all adoptions to originate with the hospital and foster care and repatriation to be directed by the DPC, which is a social welfare agency originated after the revolution to advocate for children's care.

Admittedly, the DPC officials and private social workers said babies would stay in the hospital much longer than if Sanda had those same babies, and eventually they would become institutionalized if they weren't placed in foster care.

Sanda had begun her work by studying psychology at university before the revolution. Choosing psychology for a career path under the Communists would be considered somewhat defiant in those times. In a managed society, you were expected to choose a hard science to support the economy. It was where the most openings to a comfortable life were being offered by the State, and most students followed that path. A person's soul belonged to the State, if the soul existed at all. The suggestion of freeing a soul to choose for itself could lead to questioning the State's authority over that life. Psychology wasn't needed in hard sciences; it was academia's stepchild. In twenty years, I've yet to have the nerve to press her as to why she chose the subject for her degree.

Her nursery and her willingness to help Chi Ro were an outgrowth of the holocaust she suffered through working in the State's program of supported childcare. Only recently has the term been allowed to surface in Romania. I believe it's a way of people at last expressing their sadness over what happened to children in their country

I used it on one occasion when I was pressing Sanda about her work experience in an orphanage in the town of Navodari. We had some extra time one day, so she drove me out to see it and recollect herself as I asked more questions about her work experience. As we drove past the building, she spoke of her colleagues and the respect they shared for each other caring for the children. She allowed herself to go far enough to describe these beautiful children, and she described their staff's willingness to create a semblance of a normal childhood that might encourage the kids to develop their skills to learn and grow. The kids would be evaluated as they went along, but when they reached a certain age, she said, "the doctors would come in their white smocks and stethoscopes, and they would look at the children's records and examine them. The doctor would say, 'Well, this one has good marks but has a limp. Or this one has astigmatism.' It could be anything because they were trying to find reasons not to send kids on for more training, and they would stamp the perfectly normal child's records unfit for further resourcing and they would be sent away to the Camin Spital to go crazy and die."

I asked her, "Were they limited by budgets? You know, people were encouraged to have more children, and the system just had too many kids to support that year?"

"Yes, and the budgets would change, and we never knew how many would be kept or how many would go."

In that moment I gently asked her, "Sanda, would you go so far as to say that that's the same thing that happened on the docks at Auschwitz?"

"Yes," she said. "It's the same thing." That was her pain. I took it as a gift from a dear friend.

In fairness, there is a difference in comparing the two state-sponsored programs of Romania and Germany and characterizing Romania's as a holocaust. The purpose of one was for the systematic elimination of life. Romania's program under Ceaușescu was the State-sponsored requirement for its citizens to create life. Where it is fair to characterize both as holocaust was at the moment when the State should decide who should live and who should not. In that abuse of authority, they are the same.

My friend is a stoic. Some have even said she is cold. Her

expression didn't change throughout our conversation at her former workplace. In that moment sitting with her in the car, I was twenty years into my experience being in Romania, and that was the first and clearest acknowledgement from anyone of what had happened to so many children's lives. She was not overcome. Her resolve to return kids to their families or find them foster families is born out of the disappointment of having invested in children and then experienced the absolute authority of the State to snatch them away. She would have abhorred this part of the narrative. She didn't want to bruise the State authorities who gave her freedom to move about among the needs.

When she said yes to helping us, she didn't come over to CVN with a program; she came to sit in on our meetings and watch us. In Romania, she is a cultural anomaly. If the entrepreneur is a jack-of-all-trades and the master of none, Sanda's management structures are an example of someone who recognizes a need and assembles a staff with the expertise to handle the problem. Then she gets the team moving and steps out of the way. The result is empowerment of the staff. That is not Romanian culture. For our staff, it took some getting used to it and for a few, one of Sanda's "cold showers."

From within our staff at CVN, we asked ourselves, "Who would you seek out to work as a team placing kids in homes?" The first to come to mind was our administrator, who had prepared meticulous records on each kid. Her records told us that some of our kids had families living in the area, some had parents who'd been told they were dead, and some were truly orphaned. She would become the record keeper, and there are none better. Romanian documentation is overwhelming. She takes it on with the zeal of a chemist, breaking it down until it's perfect. Too perfect.

Another staffer at CVN was initially skeptical. "Hud," she once asked in a general meeting, "where are we going to get the resources to start a placement program?" This particular mama is the oldest daughter of the couple from the Baptist church who took Greg Ogden and me in on our first visit in 1992. Trained in accounting, she was working at Coca-Cola in Constanta when Casa Viata Noua, as Adi said, gave her heart a call. She became a mama at the house.

When Sanda began assembling her team from the staff, she asked to help them find families. Adi has described this woman as a bulldozer. She would get the job done, no excuses. She became the point person at identifying potential families who expressed an interest in fostering and qualifying their willingness. She would follow up with visits to ensure that the families and children were connecting properly. The kids would run to see her in her little office. They called her "Domana Plasament," or "Madam Placement." "Domana Plasament, find me a family too!" and she always comforted them by telling them she would try very hard to find them someone.

Sanda and her staff found help at the Department of Protection for Children (or DPC). Chi Ro needed an officially licensed social worker to sign off on the foster settings. A young woman joined the team to participate in the vetting and documentation.

In the few years following the revolution in 1989 when so many Romanian parents were discovering their children's hidden HIV condition, Constanta became a very small town. Those parents began to talk to each other. As you can imagine, a few parents were unafraid about confronting their children's need for acceptance and getting help for themselves and their kids, and others weren't. Our administrator called me to tell me, "You won't believe this, but a couple with two children came to CVN today to ask to take a child." She explained to me that this couple's children were both typical, bright, handsome kids but one of them was HIV-positive. That child was in a local elementary school being ostracized by the parents of the other children in the school. They demanded the school authorities remove the child to protect their children. The mother confronted the school staff and the other parents in her village in a general meeting, admonishing them that they, too, probably had children infected by the State with HIV, and they just didn't know it or didn't want to find out. Her courage awakened the other parents to the extent of the tragedy.

This mother had originally joined the staff at World Vision Constanta to help other parents become educated about the problem, and by networking with each other, they helped destigmatize the disease. It was through World Vision's work with the DPC that she learned about CVN's need to place children. What drove this wonderful couple to foster an HIV-positive child was empathy; their family knew how our children felt, and they wanted at least one of our abandoned children to find acceptance. They hoped their own infected child would find comfort in the company of another child. And they wanted their community to witness their love for their children, no matter whose they were.

They came to the house to visit the children. They found a girl and took her home. The administrator called me again. "You're not going to believe this, but they want two children. They discovered the closeness of the two girls and how it hurt them to be apart. They want both of them."

We were not always able to place a child into a foster family before they reached eighteen years of age; however, when they reached that age, we were required to notify parents that their child existed and was in our care. As the placement process moved on and the team gained momentum, the administrator's records revealed the existence of two of our kids' families. One family had abandoned their child into the system, claiming at the time to be unable to support their child. The other family wasn't aware their child was alive. Did they wish to repatriate with their child?

Letters were sent to these parents. The team followed up with visits to one family, who was poor and nearby. They made phone calls to the other family because they lived in the west side of the country—at least a day's travel away. Years had gone by. Reactions to news like this vary; people are different, and the reasons for abandonment of these children were different. I tried to imagine what mine would be to deepen my empathy for what was to come. When the parents came to visit CVN to discuss the possible repatriation of their children, the drama in those meetings was a deeply poignant reflection of those emotions.

I witnessed the opportunity to bring mercy and grace into the lives of two children and their mothers when the mothers came to the House of New Life to find their children. One mother had taken her child in for a well-baby check as an infant, and the child had become infected with HIV, having been inoculated with a tainted serum. When her child displayed unusual symptoms, she took the child back to the clinic for an explanation of the child's condition. Recognizing their mistake, the clinic nonetheless required the mother to leave her child for further examination and later informed her with regret that her child had died. The child was forwarded to the orphanage system, where we found him at PC#3.

The mother took a train across the country to meet us and her child to decide if she could repatriate the child into her family.

"My child can't possibly be alive after all this time, or I would have been told. I was sent a letter informing me he was dead, and I went back to the clinic and they told me in person that yes, he was gone. How is this possible?"

"Madame, with deep respect and regret, your child is alive. He has been here with us. It is your decision to make if you wish to return with him to your family. If your decision is that he cannot return with you, be assured we love him and will continue to care for him as if he were our child. But the decision is yours. He is your child."

"I want him, but my husband refuses to allow him to return. We have closed that chapter in our lives, and we cannot bear to tear our hearts open again. He denies he has a child from that time."

The child came into the room to observe the finalization of the discussions. He was desperate to return to his family and wanted to hear with his own ears his mother say she could not take him back. One of the saddest experiences in my life was walking this poor woman to the front door of CVN and watching her stooped frame and defeated demeanor walk down the street away from her child toward the train to take her home.

The other child's mother came to CVN, and we met in a little office. The mother was weeping uncontrollably when her child came into the office. The child at first tried consoling her own mother. "Mommy, don't cry. Don't cry, Mommy!" Then quite unexpectedly—or perhaps expectedly—she began to hit her mother in the shoulder, crying out to her, "Mommy, how could you leave me, how could you leave me!" The team eventually returned the girl to her family, where she remains to this day.

It may seem strange, but the joy of this House of New Life is experiencing the heartbreak of seeing your children leave the house. As the kids began to go, we missed them.

As the foster care team began placing children in homes,

Cynthia and I went out to the villages and towns in the surrounding countryside or into Constanta to see where they were and how they were settling in with their new families. As she had pointed out to our first director a few years before, Sanda and her team had used their noses to match our kids with families that fit each other. There were some arrangements that didn't work out. Some died in foster care. Kids who could live independently left early. Their outcomes have been mixed. Three were returned to their parents; two of those worked out. Some connections were eventually made after difficult starts. In some cases, now after twelve or thirteen years into their placements, there is a filial bond in these families, almost as if they have become adopted.

When Cynthia and I came back to see them for the first time after their placements, I thought PC#3 would be merely a memory for them. We found them with single parents or families in every kind of residential venue you can think of. Some were in apartments in Constanta or in homes in the small towns or suburbs outside the city. To reach them in the countryside, we'd drive out to the villages outside Constanta where we found them surrounded by vegetable gardens, pet dogs and cats, and barnyard animals, chickens, ducks, and geese.

In my excitement to see them again, perhaps I was expecting the kids to run to greet me as they used to do when I would come for a visit to CVN or PC#3. But on these first visits, that was not the case. Without fail, when they saw me approach, they hung back. Some even cried. Verbal or nonverbal, in keeping with their natures, each one wanted to know, "Why are you here? Are you going to take me back?"

"Oh, no, honey. I came to see where you are and how you're doing. I came to say goodbye."

"Oh! Do you want to see my room?"

Epilogue

*And He will wipe away every tear from their eyes; and there will
no longer be any death; there will no longer be any mourning, or
crying, or pain; the first things have passed away …
And He said, "Write, for these words are faithful and true."*

—Revelation 21:4-5

A few years ago, the House of New Life moved to the suburbs.
When someone either foreign or domestic does a good work and
in the course of so doing improves the real estate they work out of,
it is customary that the governing agency finds a way to reclaim it.

But in our case, as the result of the hospital's taking the
building back, Chi Rho's circumstances improved. Once again,
our good Father made an even better way for His children. A
friend who managed the international relief efforts for an
evangelical foundation offered to give us a house they had built
for some orphans in the emerging suburbs of Ovidiu. We agreed
to share the space with their children, and Chi Rho cared for
them along with our ten remaining kids. Their children, who were
there first, were all higher functioning, and they all eventually

moved away to live independently or passed away due to complications from HIV.

The house sits on a beautiful piece of land overlooking a large freshwater lake. From the yard, the Black Sea and Mamaia can be seen across the lake in the distance. It has a large yard with cherry trees and room for the covered picnic table where the kids eat their meals outside during the warmer months. The mamas plant flowers, and the kids have room for pets. It's idyllic because the mamas have made it so.

The staff is a gift. They work cohesively and have performed miracles. They took special needs kids through puberty in close quarters. They did their laundry, potty-trained them, managed their emotional outbursts, dressed them, celebrated their birthdays, dried their tears. They've said, "We have our differences, but we get over them. We love these children and each other." One of our board members once commented to me, "You care for the staff as much as you do the kids." It's true. The rest of us think they're saints.

As time has passed, only eight remain in the house. They are very fragile. Only two are able to speak. They're in their early thirties now, still with Mari, Dorina, and others who've known them from infancy. They are of a large family, each one a unique individual.

Reaching this age for some of them was totally unexpected. This is because of the care they have received from the marvelous women who have worked with them every day for the past twenty-three years. They'll always be of smaller stature because of the virus. Mari, the special education teacher, has what I call her "Magic Room," where she performs her tricks with crafts. She's amazing; she has them creating artworks with the leftover materials, seeds, and plant life. I have some of their works on my office walls to remember what was required in order for me to have that artwork on my walls. Had PC#3 not become CVN, those works would have never appeared.

They eat well. The cooks turn out delicious soups, stews, chicken, pork, French fries, rice, potatoes, cucumbers, tomatoes, breads, cakes, casseroles, yogurts, fruits, and vegetables in season … all the foods they love, and lots of them.

The good news has been the Romanian community's growing acceptance and compassion for the people with special needs that they find among them, many of whom are the survivors of the childcare system. I think their slowly increasing acceptance by the Romanian people has been because of more compassionate influences from the West. Outsiders have brought with them customs and practices that they considered normal, and those beliefs have gradually been absorbed into Romanian society.

The impetus for my coming and returning so often was because the old model at PC#3 clearly wasn't working. And it was mostly because of the lack of exposure to and willingness to try new and different techniques.

Soon after we opened CVN, I insisted they get the children out of the house where they had been virtually incarcerated. The kids and the staff needed exposure to new methods of socialization by getting out of CVN to see the wider world. The staff needed to change up the old habits and care models and become serious about caring for the kids as if they were our own. And I felt exposure of the kids to the Romanians would accelerate the locals as well as the kids in recognizing an obvious social obligation to each other. It took a while because the staff did not want to be embarrassed by the kids' behavior, and it was extra work. The kids did not want to go because each time they had gone in a car or van they had been terrorized by the hospital staff's rough treatment. But eventually the wider world they had always viewed with curiosity through barred windows in the past was slowly becoming a nonthreatening new arena to explore.

There was resistance by the staff. Ethnocentrism is a reality no matter how gentle the entreaties. Despite the resistance, I insisted they go out. While the learning curve was steep for the kids, the staff, the people on the buses being greeted by the kids, and the customers at McDonald's or the aquarium, and everyone resented it at first, they all began to catch on. Now it's common for them to go out. They even took vacations in the Carpathian Mountains, to a town called Sinaia, which has a summer festival. We rented a villa, some of the staff went along, and it was a big summer excursion. Some of the shopkeepers in the town welcomed the kids back each summer with treats and toys and tears of welcome. They missed seeing the kids come to play.

The neighborhood has grown up around CVN. Ovidiu has become an upscale neighborhood where wealthier residents of Constanta build summer houses, and the neighbors welcome our home. Occasionally people will drop in to bring us foodstuffs, toys, blankets, and all manner of donated goods. One well-dressed woman in a Range Rover comes regularly to leave large donations of food but will not give her name. Church groups come to visit and play games or sing with the kids, and everybody's happy or in tears when they leave.

A few years ago, we donated an income-producing building to Chi Rho. We sought a plan to take the pressure off fundraising to continue supporting the work in perpetuity. Should there be a need to care for the kids after we were gone, the foundation would be self-supporting. The IRS contested the gift, and after six years, the case appeared before the D.C. Circuit Court of Appeals. The judge told the service he would rule in their favor but advised them to reach a settlement with Chi Rho. We had told the court we would appeal to the Supreme Court, and the judge agreed we would win at that level, so the IRS, as part of the settlement agreement, allowed us to sell the property and not tax the gain. The money is managed by a firm in Spokane, Washington, in close cooperation with the Chi Rho CFO. For her part, Cynthia manages a successful child sponsorship program, and faithful donors have been contributing to that effort since 1998.

Despite the Romanian government's periodically increasing payroll withholding taxes and health care benefits on the staff's salaries, Chi Rho remains sustainable, which means the kids and staff continue to be safe. Chi Rho is the one remaining foreign foundation in Constanta County caring for the remnants of the prerevolutionary orphanage system. When I called our embassy in Bucharest to complain about the increases and requested that they encourage the Romanians to allow us to accrue the benefits paid by not-for-profits, a young woman explained the increases were necessary to keep up with the interest payments due the EU to service its loans to Romania. Romania's GDP alone couldn't support the debt.

"Why don't you encourage the government to go after the 80 percent of the national economy that's black market?" I challenged. "They don't pay any corporate taxes, and you're driving away the foundations. They're leaving the country."

She said simply, "It's regrettable."

There have been other changes as well. My friend Adi has passed away. Sanda died suddenly while on an errand for the house. They both were inestimable servants, and we miss their laughter over countless lunches and dinners very much. It would be difficult to find two more Christlike figures.

Vero has retired to care for her husband, but she will

occasionally drop by to visit and catch up with her friends and cut the kids' hair. The next time we visit CVN, she has promised to come by the house and have some of our wonderful cook's grilled lunches with us.

So, having experienced all of this, can I not say we worship a God who loves each of us beyond our mortal ability to take in? Still, if we try to take Him in, as much as our hearts will allow us to, our lives will be changed. Mine was. He will open our eyes to His heart, and if we're obedient, He will lead each of us into some unimaginable circumstances and outcomes. Then the words of the prophet Micah will leap from the pages of His Word and sear themselves into our hearts to comfort, inspire, and affirm us that He will go with us to the places He sends us and show us amazing things. I saw Him do it!

Shepherd Your people with Your scepter,
The flock of Your possession
Which lives by itself in the woodland,
In the midst of a fruitful field,
Let them feed in Bashan and Gilead
As in the days of old.
"As in the days when you went out from the land of Egypt,
I will show you miracles."

—Micah 7:14-15

A Note from the Author

I want to finish with a short story. In the midst of my work in Romania, I visited my mother in Arizona. She asked me to pray with her, so that she might receive a faith like mine. We were a churched family. We were regular Sunday school and church choir people. It was on a day when I was alone with her a month before she died. We were planning my parents' move to a managed care facility and as we conversed, she suggested I should write a book about her side of the family's agricultural, political, and monetary accomplishments.

I said, "No, Mom, there's nothing in this family worth writing about. Apart from some few worldly accomplishments, it would read like a Greek tragedy. There was substance abuse, divorce, infidelity, child abuse. It's not a story worth being told."

Then she said to me, "So, how do you explain your life?" That was shorthand for "How were you able to emerge with so strong a faith rooted in the love of Christ for others?"

I somewhat misquoted Romans 8:28 to her to make a point. "Mom, I believe we worship a God Who does all things for good." Her understanding was instantaneous. That was her moment of looking back on her life and without having to explain the words any further, we both understood her sins and how I had been redeemed of the abuse to be able to share God's amazing love in such a remarkable setting as PC#3.

Her next words were, "I want a faith like that. How do I get that?"

I laughed. "Oh, that's simple. You pray and ask for it!"

She asked, "Would you help me pray to know and receive that kind of faith?"

"Of course." I walked over to her and put my hands on her frail shoulders and asked God to fill her heart with an awareness of how much she was loved.

Peter's impetuous act of walking on the water to reach Jesus must have been a childlike act of affection. As his heart leapt with love, he was momentarily oblivious to his commonsense human limitations as well as the dangers of the circumstances, and his body followed his heart without hesitation. And so it was with me as I came forward without hesitation to put my hands on the shoulders of my mother in an act of love for a tortured soul in need of peace. That act could not have been born of my natural self.

There is mystery at times that surrounds certain events in our lives of faith. There are some events that we often step back from in surprise to reprise them vicariously. If you're like me I'll reflect back and ask "Was that me who did that?" In my experience, it's always after the fact, and the outcomes are implausible; but still, they're joyful. As when the apostles on the road to Emmaus didn't recognize the resurrected Jesus who walked along with them talking about His own resurrection. But then as they ate with Him later that day their eyes were opened, and they were joy (filled).

I believe it was the resurrected Christ who lives in me, by faith, that came forward eagerly, in love, to put His hands on my mother and pray with her. Is that a mystery? For those of you who share my faith in a living God, no, not at all.

Appendix

What follows is the account taken from the notes I took during a rapidly paced monologue with the first director. These are her thoughts; the words in italics are background information from me. Names that follow staff assessments refer to the children.

FAMILY 1

Flori (staff)—*(Flori was from the old PC#3 staff.)* She is doing well. Removing Savinci, a very troubled disruptive, higher-functioning girl, was good for this family. Flori's husband has lost his job. She is focused. Her favorite child is Petra. Petra loves Kid's Club; she's learning to be a child. Flori encourages her.

Vero (staff)—*(Vero was also from the original staff at PC#3. She was the first to ask for an interview.)* She is superb: she motivates other mamas, she needs to be more flexible but has leadership potential, brings new ideas, very organized, encourages Flori, very united with Flori. Vero is a good supervisor, not management. Flori and Vero communicate well with staff, but their style is old school, very dictatorial.

Stefan—He has changed after Savinci left, no bad language, settled into the family. He loved VBS with Ken Merrifield's team from the US, and he thinks he'll go back to his original family of origin that gave him up to PC#3 when he's 18. He is never sick. His health picture doesn't match with his viral loads, they are so high. He's number 1 in school. He and Vale the teacher do well together. Like the other children, he doesn't know what to do with love. He and the others don't trust it as unconditional, and he gets angry when he experiences it. He leverages love well and easily overcomes anyone trying to give it who has poor boundaries.

Maria—She's going to have a hard time growing up. She's simple-minded and will need protection. She wants to be a cook when she grows up and clean for her mamas. She's never cried except when she was celebrated with her own birthday cake. She has a narrow range of emotions, goes into the fog, can be very happy, and always wants to please.

Alin—He's very excitable—the opposite of Maria. Has a wide range of emotions, very caring, sensitive, mediocre-to-poor health and heart issues.

Petronela—She's doing well physically, probably because she's getting enough to eat of what she wants. She's had fewer infections; she knows what she wants but is unable to speak. She says a few basic words or sounds, "pa pa, ta ta, mama."

FAMILY 2

Maria (staff)—Nonstop verbalization. Admits to being abused by her husband, has a son who loves her and hates his father. Dad drinks. She's very connected with her family of kids at CVN. She's a good mom. Very practical, sews, makes the kids slippers, a perfect mom, teaches the girls to sew, uses her brain. Florin Belascu adores her; they are linked. Her weak point is she's too involved and could burn out. She spoils her children with money she doesn't have. *(She was eventually dismissed for beating a girl.)*

An aside: We have a policy at CVN, and it is firm. If you strike a child, it is automatic and immediate dismissal. Unfortunately for Maria, she was an adult with a history of the kind of neglect and abuse from childhood that we were confronting in our kids. Our kids were accustomed to expressing symptoms of Reactive Attachment Disorder to attract individual attention from a caregiver. Abuse and its symptoms are expressed by all ages in Romania. Whether from children of orphanages or perpetuated in unhealthy families, abuse was not acknowledged. Before the revolution, the State didn't encourage therapeutic psychologists; it wanted college degrees in engineering and hard sciences. No one knew they were dysfunctional; they just assumed beatings to modify rebelliousness were normal.

We were sure other mamas hit their kids, and we knew they covered for each other. Unfortunately, staff leadership didn't recognize their own dysfunction and were afraid to lose mamas for fear of being unable to replace them. Maria had Deda in her family, and leadership failed to recognize the explosive nature of Deda as a catalyst for abuse. One of Adi's daughters witnessed more than one event and reported it to me. We examined Deda. She had welts in the shape of palms on her back. Maria denied hitting Deda, but said if she had struck Deda, Deda deserved it. Deda, while sobbing, denied it happened, protecting her mama. In her next breath she said it had happened. I encouraged leadership to dismiss her that day. They resisted. When we insisted and Maria left the House that afternoon, the reverberations resounded in the House.

Later that night at dinner, a staff member asked us, "Why do Americans not believe in spanking?

Brandusa (staff)—A bit aloof, just getting to know her, never really know what she's thinking. It's a job for her, but she has solid boundaries. Good balance with private life and work.

Deda—Sexually abused by a female volunteer, she romanticizes about knowing her mother, longs to belong. She has no concentration in school, needs adult approval, but now she has peers to relate with. She's close to Claudia. Has good health, recurrent herpes, she's a survivor. (*In the orphanage culture, survivor is a defined term. It means that despite their circumstances, no matter what they suffered, they will choose to live.*) Deda is a great manipulator, is good until after her birthday, does well in her family unit, is linked to her mamas.

Sabrie—Oh, love her! Very sensitive, mothering child, cleans up Florin, she'd rather do that than homework, behavior, and language at times. Compliant, good girl, so loving but not a fighter for her life, loves her family and mamas.

Bumba—Huge change—has really come out, loves dark glasses and mirrors, loves to sing to himself. Titus and Bumba are caring brothers. Bumba is a nonstop talker, very secure in his family. Not a survivor; he will need life care, loves his family.

Titus—Desperate to get his legs working, has walking problems, can't bend his legs from too many injections (has scars) or from being bound as an infant for too many years. Could use corrective surgery. Quieting down, loves to eat, likes his clothes, is loving and demonstrative, language skills are poor, would sit with a Walkman all day, loves music, concentration levels with all the kids is increasing.

Florin Belascu—The bed baby. Still loves his bed, he will lie there on a rubber sheet for hours if you let him, wetting himself and self-stimulating inappropriately. He loves Maria, fixates on one or two toys, much oral stimulation with his toys, just starting to chew food, ignores food that requires chewing but will eat a Big Mac. He will need life care, hates going to the bathroom, the only kid who wears diapers, physically underdeveloped.

FAMILY 3

Good *(The director liked this family)*

Sefa (staff)—I like this lady. She has good leadership skills, very quiet, very assertive character through quiet leadership, great mama *(especially for a single woman)*. Works well with Gabi, want her back, she's on maternity leave. She's not a typical Romanian; resolves conflicts with others, doesn't gossip, and finds a third party if she can't solve a problem herself *(it's rare though that a problem gets this far)*.

Lili (staff)—*(Liliana, sub for Gabi.)* Doubles as Gabi's personality. New believer, kids like her.

Gabi (staff—)Very strong personality, loving, very prayerful with her kids, proud of her kids. The kids don't understand why her husband, Adi, doesn't sleep with the other mamas.

Antoanetta—Health-wise the cyst on her liver is the same size. She needs medication for a year, but they won't operate here. A blow to her abdomen could rupture the cyst, and an infection could kill her. She's aware of this. She's very bright. She's the one who cares for her natural mother; mother is very simple. A twin brother died here at PC#3. We let her go home gradually starting on weekends if her family will allow her to come home. Began therapy work on her feelings, like most of the kids she can't identify her feelings. She would prefer to go home to Mangalia, doesn't like being here with "handicapped" children. She uses emotions to manipulate adults.

Coca—Hates her real name, she prefers the nickname Coca. She's had fewer crises over the months, couldn't express her feelings so she cried frequently. Now she's more settled and is full of life due to her connection with men, seeks them out. Adi is her main interest. She was loved as a baby, came here in 1994. Her mother died of AIDS and dementia. She has a father somewhere. Adoption proceedings have started to send her to Britain. She fits in a family. She can make her needs known as she was not neglected as a baby. She grew up in a stable manger where she was found by authorities. Doing well, she is able to express herself.

(Coca was one of the highest-functioning kids. She was unable to stop hitting other kids. The weakest kids would walk by her, and she would sucker punch them. I sat her by herself after one incident when I watched her knock Adi Secure flat. While sitting in a chair, she attempted to knock herself out by slamming the back of her head against the wall. When she refused to stop trying, I asked her to go to the director's office with me to break her pattern. She refused. When I picked her up to take her, she

erupted, kicking and screaming uncontrollably. She was tested and turned out to be non-HIV. She was much bigger than the other children.

The director encouraged her adoption to a British family who visited CVN from her church in England. When we called and spoke with her several years later, she did not remember any of us—CVN or PC#3. She spoke English with a British accent.)

Alina—Still steps back from you if approached quietly, but a lot better. She's more communicative, demonstrative, and more interactive with her peers *(the most affected by institutionalization).* You can tell she's an original from PC#3. She's coming out, no need to protect herself, loves to kiss, seeks you out.

Tita—This kid … he's an old man in a kid's body. He tries to be good, but he's a liar. "I'm sorry," but then repeats the lie. He breaks things and blames others. He's on a behavior chart. But he's loveable. He's desperate for a phone and a remote-control car. He had one for a day but broke it trying to figure out how to work it. He's a survivor but couldn't survive in the world on his own. His health is not good, he hates school, won't give a reason when asked, strong-willed, cries before he goes to school, destroys whatever he's given.

Florin Farcas—Dear me, this kid's disturbed, Hud. He sticks to you, wipes his nose on you, and then leaves you alone. He has chronic sinusitis. He understands his moms and educators and listens to them but stays in his own world. Wets his bed *(30 percent-40 percent still wet their beds—it was 80 percent).*

FAMILY 4

Gigi (staff)—I'm not sure I'd keep her on. She's a troublemaker. She cried constantly after Ferdi's death; Savinci comforts her about Ferdi. She gives Dani a hard time and gets stressed. I've coached and counseled Gigi—I advised her she's on the bubble. I've advised our administrator about her status. She loves the kids, but she's too tough on them—"old school"—expects them to respect her rather than earn it; she's proud. She "lost it" when Ferdi died. Maria came to help her—she misses him.

Will do a Myers-Briggs ASAP for all the staff.

Savinci—She's a nomad, going from family to family interfering. She will stay here until her dad comes back. She's had a spot bleed. I would let her go home but feel her dad will abuse her sexually. *(She had several acting out incidents while I was there. Threatened suicide with scissors, threatened others at the same time, swears, pushes Narcis or other kids who used to display evil acting out but are now less affected, she swears at the moms. We prayed over her.)* "Bright button" in school but no motivation. She's settled well into Family 4—good verbal balance with nearly all verbal family. *(Family concepts are foreign to our kids. They need sex education; the director will train the moms how to teach the kids. Romanians don't start educating kids on the topic in school until age thirteen. For Deda, Selda, and Stefan it's time.)* Because she's bright, she baits all the staff. She was sent to the hospital with Stefan for three days to be disciplined. She was hitting Petra, was defiant. The doctor okayed her to stay for the weekend. Stefan was more contrite, Savinci was sullen and lipped off to the nurses for three days. Stefan came home after one day. After Ferdi died, they put her in Family 4. She never wants to go back to the hospital. She wanted Mama Daniela. She connects well with Dani Radu. She was old when she came to care—nurture vs. nature? Borderline healthy; she is getting zoster herpes under her armpits.

Ionella—Needs corrective eye surgery. I feel sad for her. A moaner, she whines all the time, bad language skills. She will focus her attention on her birthday. She loves to wash the carpet, will wash them every day compulsively. She loves paper fans— very simple minded—but the teachers say she will do well in her group. Because she whines, she's ignored. *(I'm concerned for her future because others will switch off to her needs.)* Self-caring and independent, she will do repetitive work.

Georgiana—Unbelievable turnaround. She's coming out of the fog and has strong artistic talents that are emerging, fantastic painting skills. She'll do a fantastic picture but be unable to do the same one again. She sees colors and images no one else sees. Then she meticulously reproduces them with any medium of paper, plants, seeds, colored pencils, or paints that fits the image she sees. She's very methodical: an unusual combination of creativeness with the ability to stay focused for hours. Loves to do housework, loves ritual but is also inspired. Her speech holds her back, she can't form words, loves her appearance, body image, hair arranged properly. She has a beautiful, loving spirit once trust is built. She remembers and acknowledges people who were kind to her. Health is okay; sickest of all the kids from a throat infection, but she can't speak to describe her condition. Her compliance is her downside. Mamas calm her; she will need to be in a supportive environment all her life.

Narcis—What an improvement in this little girl. The evil is gone. Doing well in school, joy in her heart, very excited about all the things she wants *(she makes lists)*. Was very compulsive, but now she's content. She knows now when she's doing something wrong. She doesn't hit as much. Very demonstrative now. She will be talking, then goes into the fog, a complete blank, and then she comes back. She misses Ferdi, talks about him and where he went. She threw a ball up into the air and said, "Catch it, Ferdi." She loves mama Dani, wants to go home with her. Lots of the kids want to get out and go do things. She loves Kid's Club—in that respect she has changed too. Average in school.

FAMILY 5

There's been a big change in this family with the change of mamas. Mariana and Laura were split up. Laura is now with Sylvia. What's amazing is that they were like robots, all angels, all dressed alike. Laura has no problems now relating to the other mamas. Made Mariana a substitute and elevated Sylvia from a substitute to a mama. By doing that we opened a can of worms. Had to counsel Laura about behavior with colleagues. Young mamas couldn't handle her, put a time limit on it. Dug into her past, still meeting weekly. Dad was abusive to Mariana and her mom. Lili does the translating and is excellent. Laura needs better role modeling but is interested and relates well to Sylvia. It was tough on the kids to split up Laura and Mariana, especially Selda. Both women have huge stresses.

Sylvia (staff)—Sylvia's house is being sold to clear debts. They will move to an apartment. Sylvia comes in and counsels the other staff. *(Note: It was during these first years that we had many requests for financial help from the staff and other members from the church and the community. It was not possible for us to do this for the precedent it would set. If anything, we made it known that if anyone chose to serve in this ministry, either in Romania or the US, it was going to cost them something.)* Sylvia loves her kids. Laura is quiet. Sylvia is upbeat and positive, and the kids have blossomed. I give time off for stress-related issues for Laura and Sylvia. I don't want to lose staff and have to replace them, which will unsettle the kids. Absence of abuse is a good change; more changes to their living environs is unsettling and undermines trust. God is working in this situation. They study the Bible together. Sylvia's husband is a Muslim, and he condones her study because of the way her life is changing for the better. Dani, Radu, and Sylvia are getting along. Sylvia had accused Dani of being a lesbian, which is illegal in Romania.

Selda—This kid! I've been concerned about her because she is one of the older, higher-functioning institutionalized kids from PC#3. Only now does she allow herself to be hugged by Mariana. *(Mariana was also old PC#3 staff, and she was with Selda from the beginning of her life there.)* Selda is very close to Mariana. Selda thought the director didn't love her because she didn't hug her *(she does now)*. Selda beat a baby to death in the early days of PC#3. She wants care on her terms. Began some counseling with her last week; she was acting out verbally and was aggressive. Started a behavior chart. Doesn't know how to express frustration without being angry and aggressive. She picks on Crina, then lies about it. She used to mother Crina. She picked on Adi Secure as well. If she wants to hit, she's encouraged to hit her pillow and talk to her mama. Has been no hitting since then. Not hitting her pillow, she now throws it. She's angry at Mariana leaving and bottles it up. We meet with her weekly to counsel. In counseling I suggested to Selda she should share her anger with Jesus. When I mentioned Jesus, Selda became stoic. I moved in close *(inside her boundary)* and Selda sobbed, and it felt like a stone had been lifted off her. We told Selda fear was normal to experience. Her health is good. We are concerned for her future life. Since Sylvia has been there, Selda's been boisterous outside the home. At home she's quiet. She was admitted to PC#3 4/90 along with Saban. Birthday is in 1988, never has visitors, records currently reflect no known family, but she has a birth certificate.

Claudia—She has a very interesting history. She shows no emotions, there is no way into her zone. *(Here is where I disagreed with the director. I've seen her smile at me, laugh, and respond to looks and questions. She does remain on the perimeter of a group but will respond when invited.)* Never saw her smile or laugh; since the change in her family, she's much more vocal. She's also begun to snuggle, has demonstrated affection, more excitement and speaks Russian in her sleep. She is originally from Tulcea, a city on the Danube delta near the Ukraine. I like her. She weighs people out, is good in school, health is good, got a lot going for her, is bookworm, she'll do okay in the world. Wet her bed when Mariana was there but not now. Loves Crina and nurtures her.

Georgetta—We called her Geo *("Joe")*. She was admitted to PC#3 in 1989 from the city of Navodari as a baby after it was learned that the pediatric care she received infected her with HIV. Her mother remarried, visited once, the staff is encouraging Geo to call her mom periodically. They're encouraging her parents to take her home on the weekends; mom says yes, but we learned later her stepfather was against repatriation. The staff takes her to the house, but there is no emotion when coming back from the parents. She's a very bright little girl: creative, good natured, she has no problem expressing what she wants. Beautiful eyes.

Adi Secure—On a 1-10 scale of sickness, he's a 10. How he manages to stay alive is a mystery of the survivor's will power. He bleeds chronically from the eyes, ears, nose, and mouth. Nothing can apparently be done for him medically. He's had steroids, hemoglobin, and blood transfusions. Not much is known about his background. He eats non-stop but never gains weight, he's an ideal candidate to put on a supplemental drink. He's a great little fellow. He knows he's sick, he's a sweet little boy; simple things please him, no more activity with pencils and dolls. He'll be 12 years old this coming March. Saw a homosexual act in the hospital, wets his bed, very caring, loves his sisters and Crina. He gets every sickness but doesn't complain or come to you when he's sick—he's very affectionate.

Crina—Crina ballerina, Miss Coca '99. Used to pull off her diapers, now she eats her feces and spreads it everywhere. Huge progress verbally, ate only bread but is taking on more varieties of food, she grazes all day. Three out of five nights, she eats her poop. She has normal toilet activity but only just started spreading it. Oddly doesn't like messy play like in dirt or mud. She will always need care. Only spreads poop at night. She treats all her possessions roughly, loves to be rubbed and kneaded, becoming more restful. She and Sylvia love each other. Sylvia gives her too much. Doing a lot of cleaning because of her.

FAMILY 6

This family rolls along smoothly because of the stability of the mamas.

Dorina (staff)—Her countenance is different. She looks much younger now. When she had a prolapsed uterus this year, Daniela Ianorescu and I visited her in the hospital. We took her flowers. She couldn't believe the boss would come to see her. Dani explained it was Jesus coming. Dorina's more open now. She attends morning Bible study, her psoriasis is in remission, she opens up. She loves her kids, is great with Marcut, and works well with Anasioara. She comes to me with body problems. She'll share a laugh with you but won't share her heart.

(When I first visited PC#3 in 1992, Dorina and Vero were there as members of the original staff. Both of them interviewed, asking for the opportunity to stay with the children when PC#3 went out of existence. Dorina has always had a stoic and businesslike countenance. It is natural for her but is in no way an accurate reflection of her heart and her wonderful sense of humor. Both she and Vero could be stern and demanding of the kids; in a crisis, both she and Vero are in full control. The kids know she loves them, and the mutual respect is evident. When I interviewed each member of the staff recently, she said one of the most remarkable things. She said, "My face does not reflect what I feel in my heart." No, my friend, it does not—but your life does.)

Anasioara (staff)—She prefers to be called Ani. She is a special lady. Make her a manager down the road. Her spiritual side is lacking, but she's sympathetic. Great sensitivity, intuition, very bright, taught special needs kids once, she has developed Marcut;

he's loveable now. She has good taste. She balances Vero in team leadership; Ani has heart and sensitivity where Vero has heart. I love her. If I ignored her, she was quiet; it was because she was trying to please the boss. She is a pleaser and a servant. She is learning to question. She's good at budgeting and spends only for what she needs. *(Here is a stunning comment; if she were saved, I would make her the new director. She'll be a gem down the road for caring for the kids when they're out in placement because she's a good planner. She balances Vero who is more authoritarian.)*

(Note: Anasioara was found dead in her flat some months later of an apparent suicide. She was a sensitive, caring soul whom we all loved and respected. I was deeply saddened and angry at myself for missing the signs. I asked our staff how we missed those signs. The old top-down [vertical] style of Romanian management does not allow for equanimity among workers. The concept of shared responsibility among colleagues on a horizontal plane of authority is countercultural. No one shares their needs or ideas for making adjustments that might lead to improved workplace circumstances. We began making a shift away from the vertical to the horizontal model, and not only because of Anasioara's death. The best administrators didn't know the needs of the kids as well as the mamas, who'd spent their working lives with them. And speaking bluntly, the disparity in trust among the Baptist and Orthodox denominations stifles innovation. When some staff resisted innovation under the rationalization "that's not done here," my rejoinder was usually, "Everything we've ever done here has never been done before.")

Marcut—Deaf as a doorpost, love him, chronic tinnitus *(glue ear)*. Recurrent bacterial infections because of lack of treatment. Doing well—he's no longer afraid to go out in the van, and he loves to eat. Took him out in Ovidiu to break him out of the house; he was so violent, it required three people to hold him down. Now he loves to go because he has a buddy there. He's by far the vainest. He asks for spaghetti every day but is quieting down. He doesn't spit and kick any longer.

Laura—She's quieting down and working hard to get into school. She and her sister Valentina compete in school. She's not the showpiece any longer. She's learning to write. She asks all the other children to get it together if they act up in the play yard. I never see her sad; always cheerful, loves to sing. Had many zosters on her back and legs and had injections of hemoglobin lately for liver problems. She seems to be having a good life now.

Valentina—I'm concerned about this little girl. She blanks out and cries. She used to cry and cry for her mom; she does it again now. She's sick with recurrent bacterial infections and can't shake strep throat. She curls up in bed, tired of being sick. Took her out to shop and she loved it, asking questions constantly. *(Selda steals from the shops and the mama's purses.)* Does well in school, she's out of nursery school.

Florentina—Beautiful child, still sad, head down, compliment her and her head goes down even further. She's tender, doesn't pull her hair any longer, she cries when Ani leaves. Ani calls her on the phone. Like Titus and Ionella who could have corrective surgeries, there is no need to have her club foot operated on. She's a plodder, mediocre kid, gets infections, I'm concerned about her because she doesn't complain: too compliant. Talented at crafts, adapts well.

FAMILY 7

Daniela C. (staff)—She has troubled me and the assistant director, who has been good at assessing. Very immature, she doesn't know how to control her emotions. Her outbursts drain energy from us. She's a good victim. I told her to her face what's happening; I told her in picture form. She's not in denial, Lili thinks. No follow-up on her own, puts her own kids in day care center next to our flat. She's been on the bubble; she's accused of stealing an iron and spoons from us and when confronted, the spoons came back. Nurse Mirella had money stolen when Daniela was in her office. She and Gigi could be fired. She's been given another month to come around but is only coping, not learning.

Mihaela (staff)—Very impressed with her as a mom. Loves her kids dearly. She always checks with me if she has a question. She has a natural link with the girls, loves her job, and her kids love her. She never rats on Daniela.

Ancuta—Strange child. She's quite hard to assess. Vacant moments, easily upset if neglected, hits out at other children, she's apologetic if adults see her picking on others, jealous of others receiving affection, picks on younger kids. I pushed her away once, and she went nuts. She wants affirmation from adults, wants to go to school, can't describe her feelings, limited vocabulary, bad grammar, aloof, hasn't changed from childhood. O2 deprivation at birth or genetic deprivation.

Vasilica Marcut—Oh, this child! Definitely needs an eye operation. Desperate to connect but can't—on "self-destruct"—

damaged by institutionalization. Has huge emotional needs. She will sit and destroy things in front of adults. Hit out at Mihaela, couldn't restrain her, Mihaela went to Doina to help her. She said things so vile to Doina it frightened her. Doina is one of the least intimidated moms. Vasilica asked why Mihaela didn't hit her back. She was caught trying to force a mop head into Ancuta's mouth. She wouldn't talk about it without Mihaela there. The director said she's seen this happen before at PC#3. When asked in counseling if she didn't realize this was a House of New Life, she said yes, she could see the difference. A behavioral chart hasn't helped. Selda and Deda have learned how to earn stickers. Vasilica doesn't care. She loves school though and is in the first class. Crisis events occur over days, not an event. Trying to occupy her with crafts doesn't work. Bad language. Long term she needs lots of help. Adult socialization skills will be hard to learn. Always demanding, she's shocked people with her demands. Flori was asked nonstop for stuff. When given things, she destroys them. Then she comes out of it a Jekyll and Hyde. She swore vilely at Nuta. She would not apologize, but only when told to. I'd be frightened for this kid sexually in the future, she'd manipulate with it. *(Her willingness to manipulate her sexuality proved an accurate prediction.)*

Tanure—One of our caregivers describes her as a demanding child, which is strange to me. She is compliant after all she's been through. Struggles with school. She's loving and has a strong link with Mihaela, she never talks about her parents, whom she's met and visited *(unlike Antoanetta)*. She's a comic and does things with passion. 2nd class in school. She screamed at Dani and Mihaela that she wouldn't learn; she hates school. She would color all day, needs encouragement to do anything, lacks motivation. Not much to her. "I like to play." *(Dolls, play break from school, walking, simple foods.)* Wants to be a director. Depth lacking, very simple, to sponsors she says, "Have a good day!" No imagination, acts out roles, and gets her identity from others. Would be happy to sit on Mihaela's knee all day. Too compliant. Her mother is a hooker and trades in stolen cars, "a real stunner."

If we took in two new kids, I'd put them in this family. They're all compliant; other kids would push girls and moms. I've asked for two boys. There aren't that many kids left in the infectious disease hospital: only 20. The doctor is allocating them out to new group homes. *(This anecdotal comment from the director bespeaks the gatekeeper role the doctor had exploited in her control of the distribution of kids. As we were granted control of PC#3, we were told, "If they want to play with some kids, let them. They'll pay for the opportunity, and we'll all make some money." The kids are her assets.)*

FAMILY 8

Daniela (staff)—She's immature but getting on-the-job training. She's just a girl, a giggly girl, a friend of the other Daniela *(the one on the bubble)*. I have hope in this girl. Caught her hitting one of the kids on the fanny and rough handling of Scumpa but couldn't fire her because Scumpa is a hard case.

Doina (staff)—A superb mom! Has natural skills. She cares for her kids, loves them sacrificially, invested heavily in them *(Suzy, Benga, and Scumpa all love her)*. She's proud of them, invested so much; they belong to each other. She takes them out to church and her house. Suzy's coming along because of Doina. They love Jesus because of Doina. She's proud of her children and takes no crap from anyone about her kids when she takes them out in public. She's one of a few of our staff who take their kids out, unafraid to face the stigma. And anyone who cares for them is stigmatized, as well, not unlike anyone foolish enough to care for lepers in Jesus's ministry. Bottom line, the kids are a reminder of Romania's sin. They are the object of the nation's shame.

Suzanna—Suzy, what a change! She's come full circle. Couldn't get her out of the building or into a car. She'd spit, scratch, hit, and scream. Now her #1 love is Jesus. She's chatty, responsive, loving, but wants to get nestled in. She's still intense. Loves to sing, loves others unconditionally. She's upset because Benga and Scumpa can't talk, so she has other friends. She loves Dorina and Ani because they talk to her. Loves Alin, but there's another in the group, Laura. They're pals. They play roles: doctors and the dying. She reenacts things like moms and dads. Her memory isn't great, can't memorize songs. Has a little friend when she visits Doina's church in Basarabi. If Benga's getting love and she doesn't get a hug, she asks for one. Rarely hits her sisters anymore. But if Benga hits Scumpa, she protects them. She loves to talk to Adi, loves to get out in the van. She chooses her wardrobe. Loves the GAP jeans top the Becks gave her. Longs to see her sponsors. *(Note: Absent from this narrative are the hundreds of comments and inquiries the kids make about when their sponsors are coming to see them.)*

Has a thing for men, particularly men. She can assess character, doesn't embrace everyone, and begs you to come to her, but only after she's chosen you. Likes talking to the cook but at a 5-year-old level. Always on the want *(they all are to some degree)*. Never seems to be sick; when all the others are going down, not her.

Benga—What can I say, you know it all. Definite likes and dislikes, no team player. Plays on her own, likes musical toys. Still swings her head from side to side, very pretentious, won't take no. Doina has a hard time saying no to her because of her tantrums. She's inconsolable until she gets what she wants; food and clothes are the big items. Hates others getting attention. Can repeat words, likes singing, but all done on her terms. Repeats the Lord's prayer with her mom. Language is increasing with songs and rhymes; "da" is a big word. *(This may have been wishful thinking on the part of the director. In 28 years, I have never once heard Benga utter a single word.)* Suzy and Benga play tickle games, she plays with her fingers in her mouth. Likes nestling on laps like a baby. She doesn't like her bed; she sleeps on the floor. Likes sleeping with her mom, naps with her pillow on the heating coils in the floor.

Scumpa—Out of all the kids she is deep, deep, deeply mentally ill. I wouldn't like to see this girl grow up. She'll be very difficult to look after. She hits out at everyone. She premeditates what she does; she sets you up. She claws your face. She gets exactly what she wants. She's very bright, can-do repetitive tasks, but isn't progressing considering her cognitive level. She swings her head and moans, allows her moms to pick her up and love her. She's locked inside herself, grabs hair clips and glasses off people, has no boundaries. She will follow simple directions. Music calms her. She needs dental work but to keep her calm enough to do the work, and avoid risking a scratch or stick to the dentist, would require a general anesthetic. No one's going to do that here.

About the Author and the Chi Ro Corporation

Hudson Staffield is a native Californian and is currently living in Scottsdale, Arizona. He is a semi-retired commercial real estate developer and investor. He and his wife enjoy sharing time with their three grown daughters and five grandchildren.

The House of New Life is supported by Chi Rho Corporation, a 501(c)(3) nonprofit incorporated in both Saratoga, California, and Constanta, Romania, and by the founders' home churches of Saratoga Federated Church in California and Scottsdale Bible Church in Scottsdale, Arizona. The Holy Trinity Baptist Church in Constanta, Romania, is our local ministry partner. We have also received support from the European Command (NATO), Samaritan's Purse, and countless friends and family of the Chi Rho board. We are 100-percent efficient, so all support we receive goes directly to taking care of our kids.

For more information about the Chi Rho Corporation, please visit https://chirho-corp.org/.